THE NEXT CHRISTIAN EPOCH

The
NEXT
CHRISTIAN
EPOCH

by Arthur A. Vogel

HARPER & ROW, PUBLISHERS
NEW YORK

FIRST EDITION

LIBRARY OF CONGRESS CATALOG CARD NUMBER: 66-12647

B-Q

TO
G. E. V.

Contents

ACKNOWLEDGMENTS

Concluding portions of Chapter I are taken from my article, "On Man's Making the World and Himself," *Canadian Journal of Theology*, IX, 4 (October, 1963). Small portions of Chapters IV and VII are taken from my article, "Bodies, Bishops, and Unity," *The Anglican Theological Review*, XLVI, 4, (October, 1964). I am grateful to the editors of these journals for permission to make the quotations. Unless otherwise noted, all quotations from the Bible are from the Revised Standard Version.

Preface

THIS BOOK is another voice in present-day theological dialogue. I find it necessary to speak because so many of the voices we hear—frequently those which make headlines—seem to me to be *least* characteristic of the most promising tendencies of our day. An all-consuming admiration for the method of the physical sciences and the type of "easily understood" charges made against traditional Christian insights assure the popularity of some types of criticism. But although such sweepers of the rubble speak from elements found within our age, it remains to be seen if they can speak to people of our age in a truly helpful manner.

Even a slight experience in personal counseling reveals that what a person first says about himself, and what first appeals to him, often do not penetrate to the real source of his difficulty. I have had people explain themselves completely to me in my office and then, with unwarranted shame, come some days later and say that although they believed everything they previously said when they said it, they now see that none of it was true. I've had such experiences myself. We disguise our real problems with layers of self-deception and opposite-appearance. We must go through such "false" explanations of ourselves if we are finally to expose the core of our real problems, but that is all the more reason why we must not confuse easily understood first suggestions with more ultimate truth. What is easily understood and acceptable at first may be so only because it is not penetrating enough.

I frequently wonder whether or not some of the iconoclastic

Christian authors of our day attract a quick following primarily among those who—unknown to themselves—have not yet penetrated to their—or Christianity's—real problems. At least some of the enthusiasm for present-day "catchy criticisms" in theology seems to resemble the enthusiasm of a first self-explanation of the type made in a counselor's office; catchy criticism also frequently involves a Christianity that must be represented as less than itself in order to be so easily ridiculed. Many deficiencies in the understanding both of ourselves and of Christianity are no doubt due to the cultural air we have breathed since birth, but that fact does not prevent the deficiencies from being deficiencies. I for one am not against criticism, but I think Christianity should be criticized for what it is in its true nature and strength rather than for what it is caricatured to be by the hurried and uninformed.

At any rate, as I follow contemporary research, I find myself helped by insights that contradict the analyses often associated in this country and in England with the latest "new theology." I find, for example, that a transcendent God is the only kind of God there can be, that he is both necessary and meaningful. The doctrine of the Trinity, to take another example, has assumed greater, not less, significance in my appreciation of God's mystery, the more I understand the nature of human being-in-the-world.

These pages are offered to see if what helps me helps others.

A. A. V.

THE NEXT CHRISTIAN EPOCH

I

Starting Where We Are

IN THESE days Copernican revolutions are commonplace. "Epoch-making" discoveries are announced with disconcerting frequency; as a matter of fact, if events continue the way they are now heralded in some quarters, our epochs will soon have to be composed of epochs. Nothing else will be left. If that happens, we will, in fact, have done away with epochs, but we will certainly have become aware of the reality of change.

The universal presence of change in the world is not a new discovery; man's first attempts at philosophy and science were stimulated by his recognition of change and his desire to explain it. But with our increasing conquest of the world, the change which is becoming most significant in our daily lives is no longer the natural change that goes on without us; instead it is the change for which we ourselves are responsible. We are not externally prodded as the lower animals are by the natural forces within which we live; we find ourselves increasingly able to initiate the changes which most concern us. No other animal has revolutionized the life of its females by gadgets, fair employment laws, and legalized voting; no other animal stimulates its economy by building obsolescence into its products. Patterns of living change from generation to generation, and even though it is children who are most likely to shock their parents in this respect, when we look at the situation in general terms, we discover that it is man who shocks himself. Man is most amazed by what *he* does.

Most of the time, however, we do not look at ourselves or our relation to the world perceptively. We take things for granted, as the saying goes, and it is things we want to take. The ability to control ever more thoroughly the pre-existing forces of nature makes man a unique member of the world. New discoveries about the nature of reality excite and challenge us; they draw our attention outward, involving us ever more completely with the objective nature of the universe and with the nature of the universe as an object. Objectivity is the rallying cry of our day. It is the road to truth, our defense against passion, the means by which we can obtain all that is good and worth having.

When we objectively consider the universe as an object, its size and grandeur overwhelm us. So much is there, and it was there so long before we arrived on the scene! In our better moments we are overcome by these thoughts and perhaps resolve, as a result of them, to dedicate our individual and national energies to discovering still more about the universe. We may feel chastened for allowing our petty personal and international problems to take up so much of our time; if we would be truly objective in our personal and international lives, all of our problems would be solved.

Such dreams come easily to us, for objectivity is the oxygen of our cultural air—which may, incidentally, explain why we burn out so fast as persons in our society. Only through stupidity and ignorance can one deny the grandeur and awesomeness of the universe and of atomic energy. They are objects that transfix our imaginations and stimulate our emotions—but we must not allow them to confuse our thought. If we will be objective enough not to let the emotions arising from our awareness of the size of the universe and the power of the atom blind us, we will see that the atom and the universe amaze us primarily because their features are our discoveries. We are the ones who make surprising discoveries. When the whole picture is analyzed, a primacy of man as a person over nature as an object will be seen, no matter how big and powerful the object may be. Many of us are so busy trying to treat the world, other people, and ourselves objectively that we have forgotten that objectivity is first of all *our* desire, *our* goal. Objectivity exists only as our aim; thus, surprising as it sounds to modern ears, objectivity is anthropomorphic—man centered—through and through.

We cannot escape being men, for our only approach to reality can be through what we are. That may sound like a commonplace when stated, but it is a revelation when intelligently lived. The difficulty is that the most influential forces in our culture discourage our living it.

Still, all the results are not in. Increasing problems with ourselves and with our neighbors are redirecting our attention toward man. The awakening interest of the psychological profession, for example, in preventative mental hygiene indicates that we must, in the first place, consider men as persons in our society or men will only grow sick in the second place.

I believe that the truest epoch-making discoveries of our day will not be those which allow our age to be called "the age of steel," plastics, aspirin, electricity, antibiotics, cybernetics, the laser, or "the atomic age," but those which will allow our age to be called "the age of man." That statement will, perhaps, not sound very startling to some readers; let me hasten to add that when I suggest that this may be the age of the primacy of man, I I mean that this may be the age of enthusiastic, recognized anthropomorphism!

On the surface, nothing seems more naïve and despised in our day, nothing more opposed to its spirit and ambition, than anthropomorphism. Yet when we reflect upon our dislike, we must admit, if we are honest, that our attempts to avoid anthropomorphism—by the very fact that they are *ours*—are anthropomorphic. This book is an attempt to champion the cause of recognized anthropomorphism. There is no alternative to being what we are, so we might as well be on the side of reality. The anthropomorphism we espouse involves our constantly remembering who we are and what we are doing; such recollection, we believe, is the road to true humility and self-effacement.

The only limitations that are total and damaging to us are ones we do not recognize. An unrecognized limitation is all-powerful, for being unrecognized nothing we do can qualify its effect. It is an obstruction free to be its whole self and do its full work. A recognized limitation is not an absolute limitation; it is not arbitrary and irrational. We can be on our guard against it, thus making it a part of our knowledge and wresting its destructive initiative from it. Limitations that enter into our reflective calculations are not havoc-making intruders, causing us to overestimate ourselves or causing us to refuse to listen to others; such limitations are not able to strike us arbitrarily from behind. A man who has not allowed himself to be blindfolded is, when shot by a firing squad, as dead as a blindfolded victim, but legend speaks of the man who refused the blindfold as the only one who "died a man's death." Why? Because he died with maximal awareness of his situation. The illustration is not apt in all respects, for a man who recognizes his limitations is not as limited ("dead") as the man who does not, but the illustration does indicate that the desire to remain ignorant (signified here by the man who chose to be blindfolded) is even held in folklore to violate our human condition.

When we forget who we are we make insuperable problems for ourselves. Among the suggested epoch-making insights available to us today, we believe some reveal what man is with such clarity that we have a chance to be what we are with more understanding than at any other time in human history. There were (and are) times when men were spontaneously their full selves—after all, such living should be natural for them—but, for reasons we shall try to indicate shortly, in recent years it has become increasingly difficult for man naturally to be himself. It is not that he does not think about himself; it is that when he thinks about himself he ends by thinking himself away. As a matter of fact, his disappearance is not the end result of his deliberations; the terms he most frequently employs to analyze himself preclude his being himself even before he uses them. Recent work in phenomenological analysis, however, has begun to restore the human perspective to investigations of man. For the first time in many years we are beginning to examine ourselves as we actually exist in the world rather than as an a priori theory says we should exist. Nowadays the most immediate empirical evidence about man and his relation to the world is being examined in a way that shows how grotesque our self-intimidation in the name of "objective" reason has sometimes been. Now insights are being furnished us that show why we should not fear to be the selves we spontaneously want to be—and occasionally are, in spite of our theories.

Not the least, but perhaps one of the last, of our activities to benefit from the new insights into the relation of man and the universe is religion. It seems fair to say that we may be standing on the threshold of a new religious era, one in which our presently accepted order of priorities and truths will be shown to be incomplete if not based on outright misunderstanding.

Viewing the lethargic, socially established Christianity of our day, Christian authors in the last two decades have increasingly criticized the Church in a manner which once was characteristic only of "outsiders." The hypocrisy of social conformity and indolent respectability have finally caught up with Christianity, and many of its own spokesmen are now its chief prophets of doom. The institutional nature of the Church has been subjected to especially harsh criticism, and Dietrich Bonhoeffer's quest for a "religionless Christianity" has inspired some people to show their Christian conviction by disassociating themselves from the institutional Church. Men are not good judges of sanctity, but they know quite a bit about evil; thus the attempt of some well-intentioned persons to disassociate themselves from the evil they recognize in the Church cannot lightly be condemned by Christians of any persuasion.

The problem of religion in our age has been to get it to influence the everyday lives of its professed adherents. The practice of religion may, with some propriety, be its chief problem, for religion is itself only in practice. Not to practice it is to reduce it to an abstract theory, something it is not. Religion is not always easy to practice, opposed as it is by our selfish, ingrained habits; but difficulties arising from such a source have traditionally been considered "normal" and even necessary to spiritual growth. They are what the "spiritual life" is all about and why that life can be described as a warfare. Needless difficulties can be added to legitimate ones, however, when the true nature of the spiritual life is misunderstood.

When the spiritual activities of man are thought to be complete and justifiable in themselves alone, it will always be an intrusion upon them (and a burden upon us) to try to "carry them over" into the material world. Most Christians acknowledge that their whole lives are important to God, that they owe all to God and so should praise God in their bodies, but although they are ready to admit all that in theory, and although they want their lives to be consistent with their theories, they are prevented from achieving their goal by a deep enculturation that escapes their conscious notice. They are so used to relating their thoughts and theories to the world in an external way that they cannot help viewing their spiritual insights as externally related to their bodily lives. A neatness and completeness are found in our theories and intellectual insights considered just in themselves; since we derive some satisfaction from those activities in their bare state, it is onerous for us to "translate" them into practical terms. Our culture as a whole has separated the spiritual from the physical, theory from practice; it is no wonder, then, that the "spiritual" and "physical" aspects of our religious lives have also been separated.

The constantly decreasing role of Christianity in the lives of men has made it apparent that Christians are not living the life of Jesus Christ at the level he lived it and at the level he made it available to them. Christians have not been living their religion at the level at which they feel and deal in the world. Thus it is, no doubt, that their religion is of no help to them when they *feel* anxious and are *dealt* a blow. Jesus' victory has been won for us in *our* world, in the world in which we participate with all our being; he has won for us the freedom to be ourselves or he won no victory at all.

We often have difficulty living Christ's life because we make it impossible for ourselves to receive it for what it is. His resurrected life in heaven is a fully human life, perfected in all of its aspects, physical and spiritual. As God created us and redeemed us there is no conflict between our bodily lives and our spiritual lives. Many people find that difficult to believe when asked to accept it on religious authority alone; now, however, nonreligious insights are becoming available to us which show that we have a spiritual life only through—or better, because of—our bodily lives. These are the insights which we think can reactivate our religion by enabling us, for the first time in our era, to want to receive our religion for what it is. We Christians have been so busy trying to explain to ourselves and to others what embarrasses us in our religion that we have had neither time nor inclination left enthusiastically to live our redemption. The Christian religion has made no difference in our worldly lives because it has never been able to get into our immediate world: by apologizing to ourselves and to others for our religion we have kept ourselves from being religious. Only when we are no longer embarrassed at being ourselves can we begin to understand all that God has done for us in Christ Jesus.

Our new understanding of ourselves and our relation to the world forcefully indicate that we cannot be ourselves apart from the world and apart from our relations with other persons. When our openness to, and dependence upon, the world and other persons are understood, we can immediately see the absurdity of thinking that our religion can be ours in a way that makes it difficult to practice in the world and with others. The new turn in our basic understanding of religion will relocate many points in our once-familiar religious landscape. What were once thought to be troublesome details and formalistic instrusions in our spiritual lives will be shown to lie at the heart of our living relation with God. Our relation with our neighbors and the universe, the nature of the Church, the sacraments and our whole personal involvement in time and space, will be vivified and enlightened. All of these topics concern basic sources of Christian significance and power.

I see man's increasing concern for himself as a hopeful sign on the religious horizon, but that concern alone will not be sufficient to bring about the religious renaissance of which we are speaking. Motivated by our concern, we must come to a better understanding of ourselves. The immediacy and constancy of the personal and social problems, to which reference has already been made, sap more and more of our strength and take more and more of our time. The difficulties we have with ourselves, with neighbors and strangers, are now growing so prominent that they are forcing a new recognition of man's primacy as a person over his function as a thing. Psychological breakdowns and social strife are beginning to prevent us from thinking that the impersonal, objective nature of the universe should be our only concern in life.

The primacy of man as a person is increasingly being forced upon us; yet that primacy is something with which we are not prepared to deal and something we know we are not prepared to exercise. The difficulty is all the more acute, as many clear-sighted commentators have been suggesting in recent years, because, although we are concerned about ourselves, analysis reveals that we are the ones persecuting ourselves. It is our own activities that make it so difficult for us to be ourselves.

The solution to our problems awaits our realization that we can neither fulfill nor produce ourselves in any final sense by the scientific and technocratic methods characteristic of our age. Yet with a hope in the positive sciences which has become increasingly naïve as our social difficulties have become increasingly desperate, many of us feel obliged to try to live our personal lives exclusively within the world as it is defined by man's scientific activities.

The physical and mathematical sciences are rigorous, abstract disciplines whose clarity is proportioned to their abstractness. The trick we play on ourselves is to argue that, because of the type of clarity these sciences have, their abstract viewpoints must be prior to all else in reality. The uneasy situation in which many people find themselves today is the direct result of their attempt to make their personal selves coincide with, or try to live within, the abstractions of science.

Treating a person as a thing among things, looking at man as if he were only a special kind of thing, ends by making personal living superfluous and impossible. People behave differently from the material objects science studies. The fact that man has developed a science, which "things" have not produced for themselves, shows that he is basically different from things. Yet the paradoxical fact remains that in our scientific activity—in the realm in which we are obviously different from things—we frequently try totally to explain ourselves in their terms. In an area of his life made possible only by his freedom and autonomy, man thus tries to deny the true basis of his scientific endeavors.

Roger Mehl has written: "The paradox of scientific research is to require from the scientist an activity of self-effacement. Truth will be better attained in proportion to the scientist's ability to reduce his own ambitions and experience and to place himself under conditions which are an adulteration [*dénaturation*] of man's real condition. . . ."[1] Many people nowadays forget that, the results of scientific investigation notwithstanding, the "activity of self-effacement" of which M. Mehl speaks is itself an act of deliberate personal choice. The primary condition of specialized scientific thinking, taken as a whole, always depends on man as he is an autonomous person, even if some of the specific results of science do not. It is only to the extent that other people are willing to make the same antecedent choice as the scientist that they are able to recognize the formal value of scientific facts.

That we cannot actually live the formal denial of ourselves which the results of our abstract science prompt us to make, is a major source of our present malaise in the world. The anonymity which the scientific and technocratic methods foster, contradict contemporary man's most immediate experience of himself as a person. It has been suggested that man cannot help but limp if he tries to walk through life with his feet on two different levels: one the level of personal identity and the other the level of scientific anonymity.

Science puts man in a world, but it is a scientific world. There is nothing wrong with such a world; it is good in itself and much additional good can come from it. The difficulty is that, although good, it is inadequate. The insight which so many of our contemporaries lack is the recognition that the so-called scientific world is in itself a derivative world; it is sustained and found within another world prior to and more complete than it.

In one sense we do not get newer dimensions of living from formal science, but fewer. True life-dimensions are concrete, qualitative wholes which contain man as a whole. They add richness and fullness to life by offering new totalities within which we can live in the totality of our being. In its formal activity

[1] Roger Mehl, *The Condition of the Christian Philosopher*, trans. by Eva Kushner (Philadelphia: Fortress Press, 1964), p. 44.

science does not add such richness to our lives; it abstracts from that richness. The impressive development of science in recent years has not added any new rooms to the house of our lived-world. Still less has it offered us a house that is totally different from our ordinary lived-world. We cannot enter the world of science as we can a room of our house and discover new areas for personal living. Science is written on the "walls" of our lived-world and is carried on within that world; it has not put a new addition on our world as a whole or supplied us with a substitute world.

The *n* dimensions of mathematics, for example, are not new dimensions of fully personal living. They define the *limits* of our personal lives much more than they provide new dimensions for those lives considered in their entirety. The "world of science" is one into which we cannot step—it is literally a "no man's land," to use Georges Gusdorf's description—but because it gives us valid insights into certain aspects of the world in which we live, it can change what we do within *that* world. There is, however, a tremendous difference between changing what goes on within a world and changing the world itself. Science abstracts from the concreteness of the lived world; it, as a formal object, has fewer dimensions of being than the men who produce it. The attempts to derive man in his fullness from the results of his own abstract investigations is analogous to trying to draw depth from a surface, to wondering why we can't get a third dimension from a two-dimensional plane.

We must remember that man always *finds* himself in a world: a world is presented to him with his being. In some unique sense, the world in which we so find ourselves must be *our* world, for only in it can we be ourselves. What we have said is not to deny that man can change this world. There is, in fact, a two-way influence from man to the world from the world to man; the important thing is that the world which is somehow correlative with man is the only world sufficient for him.

Contemporary man has lost the nerve necessary to live in *his* world, the world correlative to his whole being. He wants to fabricate a world according to his own design, one in which he will be safe from the dangers which confront him in the fullness of reality. In man's real world he must take a chance. He must dare to be himself; he must at times morally commit himself to such a degree that there can be no compromise within his decision. Such a world is not always a place of comfort, but it is the only kind of environment within which truly personal growth can occur. Thinking that he has already grown, present-day man is more anxious to protect himself than to be himself. He does not realize that to be a man means to have a destiny at every moment which can be either won or lost.

In order to have a primacy of the person there must be a primacy of the person's world. That world is the world of values. Our major threat is to be devalued, to be shorn of value, to try to live without value. Yet such devaluation is exactly what we are doing to ourselves in the activities of which we are most proud, namely, in the physical and mathematical sciences. The devaluation of the human world by physical science has gone so far that in many quarters people think the realm of fact is totally distinct from the realm of value. If we are troubled with a question of fact, we are told that science can handle the matter. Since facts are thought to be stable and objective and since descriptions of fact are the product of science, values are held to be subjective, arbitrary opinions men project into the world. There is common agreement that all judgments about the importance of things are value judgments: to say that something is important to us is to say that it has value for us. The difficulty is that, taking all the just-mentioned views together, we are left with a position which says that what is important for man has no necessary connection with facts, and what is valuable for man can have no objective stability.

There is some truth in all the opinions we have just stated. Human values are not the same as scientific facts, but that need not imply that such values have no relation to facts or that "scientific facts" have no value in themselves. There is a sense in which the highest values for man depend upon his free decisions, but that need not imply that such values are arbitrary options. That there are facts upon which one can base a description of the proper values for man does not in any way relieve man of the responsibility of choosing those values if they are actually to be realized in him and in the world.

As an actualizer and experiencer of value man most completely escapes the bounds of science. Science has an important role to play in the deliberations from which man's value judgments result, but science cannot control those judgments by itself because it abstracts from too much of man in carrying out its own activities. The realm of value is the realm of participation; as such, it is always immediate and experiential in nature. Truly human values involve the total participation of the whole man. That wholeness transcends science and cannot be produced by science.

Value is fulfillment; it is the satisfaction and completion of tendencies. As such, value is always—and only—found at the level of living, acting being. Food is a good or has value for me insofar as it satisfies my hunger. There are, to be sure, reasons why food satisfies my hunger. These reasons can be systematized and described in the special sciences, such as chemistry, physics, biology, and nutrition. Nevertheless, these descriptions, no matter how complete and accurate, are not themselves the actual satisfying of hunger. For that reason they have no value for me as food: they are no good to me when I am hungry. As an existing subject, both I and my needs transcend abstract description. The scientific description of the passage of food in my mouth and digestive tract is a totally inadequate substitute for the goodness and value of food itself. The value of food comes from the fulfillment and actualization which it brings; that actualization is not unrelated to the scientific description of the facts, although it is certainly more than such a description. Any attempt to substitute abstract descriptions of man for concrete human value destroys man as an actually living entity; any attempt totally to separate human value from a rational description of the world reduces his personal life to blind caprice.

To discover and experience value in the world is to "belong" in the world. Schizophrenia, we are told, is the characteristic mental disorder of our day. Can we not see an obvious connection between man's present disdain of value and his feeling of not really belonging in the world, one of schizophrenia's primary symptoms? The need to "humanize the world" is, indeed, *man's* need. "Belonging" is important to us. But in order to achieve that goal we must, first of all, not be ashamed to be ourselves. Neither theological surfeiting nor scientific subtracting must be allowed to sublimate our true vocation as embodied persons.

A consensus is developing about what man's problems are, but there is as yet no common agreement about how to solve them. A consensus is also being reached about Christianity's shortcomings in the face of a nonbelieving world, but there, too, suggestions as to how to remedy the situation differ widely from one another. Many people see the possibility of a new epoch for Christianity, but they see that epoch structured in different ways. The common goal of all present-day Christian reformers, however, is to make Christianity realize its own nature and play its *effective* role in our daily lives.

I have given a brief indication of the understanding of man and his relation to the world from which I believe Christianity's next great thrust will arise. It remains for us to develop certain themes from that background more fully and show their relation to central Christian tenets. Other Christians, however, are placing their hopes in different possibilities. Some have been impressed by the work of linguistic analysis on the nature of religious discourse; some are persuaded that metaphysics (at least as traditionally held) is no longer tenable and that the methodology of the positive sciences now reigns supreme in the world; still others have reacted so strongly to Christianity's failure to speak out and change the world that they want to reduce Christianity to ethical practice pure and simple.

In order to focus my position more clearly in the end, it will be profitable now to examine some of the possibilities we have just mentioned. After we have seen the type of Christianity they would produce we will have a useful model with which to contrast my own suggestions.

I I

Against God and for the Gospel

RELIGION HAS recently been most seriously challenged in the English-speaking world by the school of linguistic analysis. According to that school, when we hear or use a religious statement (or any statement for that matter) our first concern should be, What does it mean? Linguistic analysis itself has undergone a number of modifications since its inauguration by Bertrand Russell and G. E. Moore in the early years of this century. Throughout its development, however, it has consistently championed the importance of knowing the precise meaning of what we are saying and the contention that the quest for such meaning is the proper work of philosophy. The sympathy of the analytic movement has largely rested with the experimental sciences; that sympathy is well illustrated by the verification principle of meaning which guided the school for many years.

The verification principle has itself been held with varying degrees of strictness since its first bold proclamation, but for our purposes we need consider it only in its more recent formulation. Nowadays the principle is usually advocated in its "weak" form: a statement, to be meaningful, must allow some type of specific, relevant empirical verification. A significant statement must affirm something which can, in principle at least, be checked by empirical—and ultimately experimental—operations. Stated in different words, the principle maintains that if it is logically impossible to devise a means for determining whether or not a statement is *false*, that statement is not informative. Any statement which says something, by the very fact of its affirmation, excludes something

else; if a statement were to exclude nothing, it would be incapable
of ever being wrong. Thus it would be so general that its affirmation would be insignificant and useless in our practical lives.

Let us look at a specific example of how the verification principle
of meaning works. There was a time when man had not yet seen
the back of the moon, but even then, the principle held that statements about the back of the moon were meaningful, for men could
at least specify the *type* of operation that would give them empirical knowledge of it. That operation would be to send a rocket
around the moon. Knowledge of the kind of operation that would
enable sensual knowledge of the moon's back was enough to guar-
antee the meaning of statements about the moon's then-unseen
side, even though the actual performance of the operation was
impossible at the time.

The meaning of any proposition is determined by specifying the
operations which would be performed in order to test the statement's truth or falsity in a sensually significant way. The meaning
of a proposition is not simply identified with its truth or falsity,
but a proposition's meaning does rest upon the type of operation
that would suffice to establish its truth or falsity. Statements about
the "providence of God," when judged by the verification principle, are quite obviously meaningless. Since *whatever* happens in
the world—life or death, feast or famine, success or failure—can
be called providential, statements claiming to refer to God's providence can never be proved false. Consequently, the verification
principle holds that nothing is significantly said in affirming
them.

Some kind of sensory verification is still the best criterion for
meaning in the eyes of many people, but the variety of meaning
and intention in our "ordinary language" is so impressive that
another theory of meaning, more adequate to that language, has
arisen. Ludwig Wittgenstein was so struck by the variety of linguistic uses, or as he called them "language-games," that he re-
nounced his earlier verificational view of meaning in favor of what
is known as "functional analysis."[1] The contention of such

[1] "Functional analysis," as "verification analysis," is a term coined by
Professor Frederick Ferré in his lucid and helpful book, *Language, Logic
and God* (New York: Harper & Row, 1961).

analysis is that the true meaning of many statements cannot be found by trying to translate them into statements about sense experience (protocol statements). Functional analysis maintains that instead of there being one inexorable logic for all statements, every statement has a logic of its own. The only way we can hope to understand a statement is to examine its *use* in our full daily lives. Such an approach takes a wider view of language than verification analysis does; it sees language as a human product, developing out of man's whole communal and cultural life.

Because functional analysis does not prejudge the possibility of meaning the way verification analysis does, it allows a more sympathetic understanding of religious statements than the latter. Still, verification analysis has been an important tool for clarity in many areas, and both types of analysis have impressed religious people. Religion based on a distaste for clarity should not be desired by anyone. Thus it is that the "case for Christianity" has been attempted from both of the linguistic orientations we have just described.

The view that the positive sciences now rule supreme in the world of our empirical experience, and the accompanying dismissal of metaphysics as an outmoded pastime, are so familiar to us that they hardly need explication. We live in a culture permeated by these opinions. We have all studied under teachers, from grammar school on, who knew no alternatives to them; our circle of friends can hardly avoid including a majority of people whose chief goals in life are furnished by science and technology. Christians who have reacted against their religion's indolence in the world and who want to reduce religion to ethics are relatively few in number compared to the advocates of the all-sufficiency of science, but the position such scandalized people maintain is clear enough not to require a synopsis here. They simply equate Christianity with certain "good" actions in the world.

In examining the views contending for the decisive role in the next Christian era, our task can be greatly simplified if we examine the presentation of Christianity made in a recent book, *The Secular Meaning of the Gospel.*[2] All the positions we have just mentioned may be found in it, for the author stresses the impor-

[2] By Paul M. van Buren (New York: The Macmillan Company, 1963).

tance of linguistic analysis; he accepts the absolute supremacy of science in the empirical world; and he advocates a Christianity that is completely reduced to ethics. Because many of the features of such a secular meaning of the Gospel contrast directly with my understanding of Christianity, the intention to use alternate opinions to highlight my suggestions will be handily achieved in considering this volume. All references to secular man and the secular understanding of Christianity in the rest of this chapter will be based on the views expressed in the just-mentioned volume.

Before proceeding any further I must state my sympathy with the motivation behind Dr. van Buren's book, that is, the desire to make Christianity meaningful and viable to contemporary man. We have already discovered that desire to be a common bond among all who have suggestions for the Christian community, and it is the motivation for my own endeavor. The common mind we have just described breaks down, however, when "contemporary man" is characterized more specifically by present-day apologists. For Dr. van Buren, contemporary man is secular man. No notice is taken that the secular world may be incomplete or that secular man may be deficient; the unargued assumption is that the secularization of the world has occurred and that Christians themselves are now secular people. Dr. van Buren's approach to religion is thus quite different from such men as Mircea Eliade and Georges Gusdorf, who have examined the differences between the secular and religious worlds and tried to show that the secular world cannot contain all of the valid aspects of reality religious man recognizes. It is to the description of Christianity as allowed by an at least assumedly triumphant secularism that we now turn.

How do secular people understand the Christian faith? By giving a functional analysis of what a man (a secular man, of course) means when he uses the language of faith. For such a man the traditional language about a supernatural God has died "the death of a thousand qualifications," to use a phrase taken from Anthony Flew. The problems secular man has with traditional religious terminology are not surface problems; they penetrate immediately to the word "God," the word which casts its light, or, as the secularist would prefer, shadow, upon all other traditionally religious words. "The empiricist in us finds the heart of the difficulty not in what is said about God, but in the very talking about God at all. We do not know 'what' God is, and we cannot understand how the word 'God' is being used. It seems to function as a name, yet theologians tell us that we cannot use it as we do other names, to refer to something quite specific. . . . The problem is not solved . . . by substituting other words for the word God. . . ."[3]

People who attempt such substitutions are a prime target for the secularist's critical arrows. At first sight there are a number of contemporary thinkers who would appear to help secular man, for they admit the very problem he does about the word "God." In the end, however, these people are no help at all, for they offer "solutions" that are as problematic as the problem they started to solve. "It will not do simply to translate the difficult word 'God' into some highly or subtly qualified phrase such as 'our ultimate concern,' or worse, 'transcendent reality,' or even 'the ground and end of all things.' These expressions are masquerading as empirical name tags, and they are used as though they referred to something, but they lead us right back into the problem of ancient thought, or they put us in the worse situation of speaking a meaningless language."[4]

Judged by the only empirical criteria the secularist will allow, the word "God" is equivocal and misleading; it looks like a proper name, but there is something improper about it for it does not function the way any other proper name does. Substitute words such as "transcendence," "being," and "absolute" do not solve the problem; they only evade it. Not to be like other things, for the secularist, is to be meaningless. Traditional Christian thought, we should note, stresses the difference of God from the world, that he is unique and not like anything else; traditionally, the fact that the word "God" does not function like other proper names in our language is the best thing that can be said about it, for that is the only reason it is able to designate (although imperfectly) God at all.

The secularist contends that insofar as Christianity is to be significant for him it must be expressed without any transcendent

[3] *Ibid.*, p. 84.
[4] *Ibid.*, p. 170.

reference. "God" is a meaningless word and besides that "the idea of the empirical intervention of a supernatural 'God' in the world of men has been ruled out by the influence of modern science on our thinking."[5]

A well-read secularist might take some pause at that last remark, remembering the book in his library by the priest-physicist William G. Pollard entitled *Chance and Providence*. Dr. Pollard contends that contemporary physics allows an open universe of exactly the type necessary for God to accomplish his singular work in it. Because quantum mechanics indicates that chance and accident (or better, singular, nonrepeatable events) are real aspects of nature, Dr. Pollard suggests that science has shown that the type of events that God's providential action in the world are reputed to be are basic to the physical structure of reality.

Dr. Pollard might be able to show that Dr. van Buren's secularist is poorly read in contemporary science; the very least the conflict between the two men shows is that "physicist" and "secularist" need not mean the same thing and that in this case they certainly do not. Be that as it may, the attitude ascribed to the secularist is a common one, and so the problem it presents is a real one—although perhaps a mistaken one. There are people who believe that science has shown that God cannot intervene in the empirical world. These people are willing to admit that all empirically significant statements about reality are found in, and come from, the positive sciences. The interesting thing for us at the moment is to discover how a person who adopts this view can claim to give an adequate account of Christianity in the terms left at his disposal.

Near the beginning of his book Dr. van Buren points out in some detail the inadequacies of traditional patristic thought, recent biblical theology, and existential thought, which latter he thinks is nonbiblical. Traditional thought about the Incarnation was too static; it was too much concerned about the metaphysical conditions of the Christ-event and too little concerned about the event itself. The traditional theological emphasis was upon a metaphysical analysis concerning the possibility of the Incarnation

[5] *Ibid.*, p. 100.

rather than upon the influence of the event on our lives. An anti-metaphysical secularist can obviously get no help from such a source.

More recent biblical theology has improved on patristic thought by developing an Incarnational theology in terms of "call and response." God calls man to him in the covenant he established with Israel and man perfectly responds to that call in Jesus, the fulfillment of Israel's vocation. Instead of describing the Incarnation in terms of abstract metaphysical principles, we are here dealing with dynamic, living terms: God calls man in Christ and we respond to God in Christ. Jesus is himself the personification of "call" and "response." The latter are terms with which we have living involvement. They are much closer than the patristic terms to the genuine biblical witness, but, unfortunately, the biblical terms themselves are foreign to secular ears. Our present need is to rewrite the Bible in secular terms.

As we have indicated, contemporary existential theology is also found inadequate by secular man. Existential thought says that the ultimate ground of things can be experienced by us, but such thought goes on to describe that ground in terms of "nonobjectivity." But to experience something that is "nonobjective" will not do for the secularist. "This extremely odd use of the word 'experience,' which is ordinarily used of that which can be sensed in some way, suggests a confusion of categories, a mixing of language-games."[6] Existential language is censured for being oblique and unverifiable. To an existentialist who is being chastised, however, such criticism will appear much more to expose the dogmatic espousal of sensation as a criterion of meaning on the secularist's part than as an inadequacy in the existentialist contention. The suggestion of the existentialists is that, if our experience is adequately searched, aspects of persons will be discovered that transcend sensation. "Empirical" is not synonymous with "experimental" or "sensual"; our most immediate experience contains elements—such as our basic awareness of ourselves—that exceed sensation and that cannot be experimented with as the objects of science are. Experience is more inclusive than either sensation or

[6] *Ibid.*, p. 65.

experimentation. Any secularist who finds gratification in another person's free acceptance of his views should be aware of that fact.

The last tug that pulls the rug out from under any attempt to speak meaningfully of God is found in the secular denial that "modern man" can use analogy in his religious language. Analogy is said to mean nothing to him; thus the only mode of traditional religious reference to God is dismissed by title. Unjust as all such dismissals are, we can at least understand why analogical thought about God appears unworthy of discussion to the secularist. The distressing feature of analogy is that its proponents are willing to grant "that they cannot say to what extent the analogies are apt and proper."[7] Analogical predication does not sufficiently *specify* what it is saying; its meaning is not circumscribed by our empirical operations, thus it lacks the clarity of the experimental sciences. What was once thought to be analogy's chief virtue, that it does not restrictively specify the way a characteristic is found in God, is thought by the secularist to be analogy's chief vice. *Sic transit gloria mundi.* But we can see that no other alternative is open to those who think that significant information about reality can be obtained only through experimental specification.

The verification principle rules out the possibility of theological statements having any meaning for secular man if such statements are taken as "straightforward empirical assertions about the world." But all is not lost, for religious statements can have utility and meaning if they are understood as "expressions of a historical perspective," in contrast to empirical descriptions of reality.[8] In the now-suggested view, Christianity is reduced to a certain interpretation of historical facts. The interpretation of those events, considered in itself, is called a "blik," adopting the word coined by R. M. Hare. Such an interpretation of historical reality has empirical consequences in a person's life, but, since it is only an interpretation, it does not itself claim to make empirically provable statements about reality.

Bliks are held to be nonverifiable; they are not determinable in

[7] *Ibid.*, p. 97.
[8] *Ibid.*, p. 199.

any final sense by empirical inquiry; they are not explanations; there is no arguing about them. They are actually basic *presuppositions* about the nature of the world. Faith is said to be such a blik. In so saying, Dr. van Buren notes specifically that he is asserting that faith is *noncognitive*. If faith were cognitive it would somehow have to speak analogically about something it admits to be ineffable, but to speak about what cannot be spoken about is nonsense. Because faith is noncognitive it can say nothing significant about the nature of empirical reality. It is from science that we get informative statements about the empirical world; faith refers to our basic presuppositions about life. In the end, faith is the actual living of certain presuppositions which orient our lives and all of our special activities in the world.

Such a view of Christianity avoids conflict between science and religion because in it the "Kingdom of God" can be shown to be within us in a way science can never touch. Science has full sway in the empirical world; that is why the secularist says a transcendent God cannot intervene in the world. If the empirical world has been taken away from God by science, "bliks" are the only building blocks he has left for his Kingdom. But then, one must add, since a transcendent God is meaningless to secular man anyhow, God's absence may in the end keep the loss of empirical reality to Christianity from being a loss. A God who is *nothing* can hardly lose *anything*.

We do not intend to stop for criticisms of the Christianity of the secular man at this point, but its spirit seems to be moving so far from the spirit of the Scriptures that perhaps we will be pardoned for calling attention to the contrast that is developing. In the earliest apostolic preaching of which we have record, Jesus Christ was known and recognized because of the signs he worked in the world. In any unbiased reading of the Gospels Jesus cannot be separated from the working of miracles. To be sure, his miracles were accomplished within the context of his teaching; there is even testimony that where his teaching was not accepted in faith he could not or did not work miracles. (Cf. Mark 6:1-6.) But as correlative as his signs and teaching were (and we are here taking his signs to culminate in his resurrection from the dead and his postresurrection appearances), there is no witness of any kind in canonical Scripture that he was ever accepted as the Messiah by anyone apart from the confirmation of his teaching by empirical signs. It would seem to follow for the secularist position that if people had not first made what the secularist considers to be mistakes or misleading elaborations, there would be no Christianity today to purify and translate. Empirical signs are so closely associated with Jesus of Nazareth that, if they are mistakes and we now take the mistakes out of the mistakes, we may wonder if anything is left at all.

Returning to our account of the "secular Gospel," we must note that the historicity of Easter Day is of supreme importance in it. Easter is the beginning of everything for all Christians; for the secularist, Easter enables Christianity to be historical rather than metaphysical: " . . . we are committed to a Gospel which begins . . . with the impact of whatever it was that happened on Easter in the context of a particular history."[9] "Whatever it was that happened on Easter" does not tell us much; however, it does admit that something historical occurred. Out of that historical event a blik arose, but that blik makes no empirical claim about the world. It does not even make an empirical claim that Jesus physically rose from the dead; statements about the physical resurrection of a body are empirical statements about the world and thus not the proper intention of a blik. Easter conceived as a blik amounts to no more than a predisposition to believe that our life will not end with death. Firm adherence to that belief is what grasped certain men on Easter Day, but such a predisposition says nothing about physical events at the tomb. Easter is the discernment of an attitude which is more than any physical event; in fact, the attitude itself could never be substantiated and proved by an historical event. To believe in the physical resurrection of Jesus would be to mistake an interpretation of history, a blik, with the entirely different frame of reference of statements about the empirical world.

Jesus of Nazareth was a unique person in human history. And his singularity can best be described by his *freedom*. Jesus was a good son, but free from family bondage; he kept the religious traditions of his people, but felt free to disregard them on occa-

[9] *Ibid.*, p. 99.

sion. In the accounts of his miracles he is even represented
"mythologically" as unlimited by natural forces. He taught, not as
the scribes, but with a freedom that witnesses to his own authority; he was free in his dealings with men, completely open and
receptive to friend and foe alike. He was free to associate with
anybody, not just respectable and approved people; he had no
morbid need to establish his own identity. Jesus counseled his
followers to be free also, urging them not to be concerned and
anxious about the goods and honors of this world. Because he was
not defensive, his freedom from self set him so far apart from the
men of his day that they finally tried to answer his threat to their
lives by killing him on the cross.

The historic Easter event is crucial, as we have indicated. The
secularist sees no harm in admitting that the experience the disciples had at Easter was a subjective one because every experience
must, by definition, be had by a subject. On the other hand, the
disciples' experience was also *of* something, as every experience is
by definition; in that sense it can be objective. The content of the
Easter experience was Jesus and his freedom known in a new way.
"We might say that, on Easter, the freedom of Jesus began to be
contagious. The word is used with care. It suffers somewhat from
a biological connotation, but we also use it in a figurative way:
'He has a contagious smile.' In a crowd of people, fear can be
'contagious' and produce panic. A child's laugh can be 'contagious.' It is in this figurative sense that we say that Jesus' freedom
from himself and freedom to be for others became contagious on
Easter. It carries the sense of our 'catching' something from another person, not by our choice, but as something that happens to
us. We use it to point to the event of Easter, not of course to
describe it."[10]

It is curious here to see secular man doing what we have previously been told he cannot do. The use of the word "figurative"
cannot hide the fact that the Easter event has just been characterized by analogy! Made explicit, the analogy states that as disease
may be to an organism; as fear may be in a crowd; as a child's
laugh may be to those around him; so Christ's freedom was to his
disciples on Easter Day. As spreading is to disease, so spreading is

[10] *Ibid.*, p. 133.

to Christ's freedom. Will it do to try to attenuate the use of analogy by saying that it is only being used to point to Easter, not to describe it? Hardly. The only way the word "contagious" points is by describing. The *meaning* of the analogy is vital for the secular position, and no denial can change that fact. In itself, of course, this analogy is not about a transcendent God, but it does show that the structure of analogical thought is not foreign to secular man and is even necessary for him.

When the disciples spoke of God having raised Jesus from the dead, the secularist understands that what they were really doing was indicating the fundamental role the blik they caught on Easter played in their lives: reference to "God" was their way of indicating the *totality* of the obligation they felt to live Christ's freedom. The emphasis on the physical resurrection of Jesus occurred only in the "later tradition" and meant, not that a cadaver was resuscitated, but that the experience the disciples had was an experience of the very Jesus they had known before his death. The Jesus who now lives is the historical Jesus. Because that statement is the essence of the Christian blik, the historical Jesus can never be unimportant to Christians.

As a final summary of the nature and significance of Easter, we read that two days after Jesus' death "Peter, and then other disciples, had an experience of which Jesus was the sense-content. They experienced a discernment situation in which Jesus the free man whom they had known, themselves, and indeed the whole world, were seen in a quite new way. From that moment, the disciples began to possess something of the freedom of Jesus. His freedom began to be 'contagious.' For the disciples, therefore, the story of Jesus could not be told simply as the story of a free man who had died. Because of the new way in which the disciples saw him and because of what had happened to them, the story had to include the event of Easter."[11]

We should notice that the post resurrection experiences are here admitted to have a sense content of Jesus as their object. Such an admission is meaningful from the secular point of view and does not claim that Christianity is *proved* by the sense experience. The important thing is not the empirical event that happened, but that

[11] *Ibid.*, p. 134.

the event—whatever it was—made the disciples aware of the Christian blik. The mind's eye was opened to a new perspective; once grasped by the latter, any concern about Jesus' physical body becomes a perverse attempt to substitute archaeology for religion. The minimal terms by which the event is described emphasize the minimal dependence of the event on the *kind* of sense experience involved. But that even such a minimal description is *necessary* indicates that the original discernment situation in which men "caught" the Christian presupposition occurred *only* by means of an experience that included sensual, empirical elements. In that case, at least, there would seem to have been a partially verifiable or cognitive reference to the empirical world from within the Christian blik.

We recognize that the secularist contention still does not state that a dead body was physically raised from the grave. The sense content the disciples experienced might have been some kind of projection or hallucination. From the secular point of view, the only meaningful explanation of the sense content which the biblical witness insists upon could be in terms of hallucination and projection. The secularist is sure that the sense content could not have been of Christ's physical body, for that would contradict his biological knowledge of the cellular decomposition occurring at death. It would do no good to say that God had given Jesus a new and different kind of body, for "God" is a meaningless term. If it is suggested that Jesus had provided himself with a new mode of appearing to men, we would encounter much the same difficulty, for we would be imputing a transcendent kind of causality to Jesus. Such imputation is as meaningless as "God" is. We are left with a blik whose obligation and contagion we feel as "objective," but whose only occasion of discernment, as reported by those who caught it, is projective and illusory. Again, we may simply admit that that is the way a blik may come; if that is its nature we must accept the fact. But if bliks have such a tenuous relation to the empirical world in *which they must be lived,* we may legitimately wonder how reality became so ordered in the first place. It would almost look as if the basic constitution of the world itself were schizophrenic.

The resurrection, we are told, cannot be spoken of as if it were a fact, for our "factual terms," taken from the positive sciences, cannot apply to it.[12] That is not a great loss, however, for the mere fact of the resuscitation of a physical body would not itself demand the response of Christian faith. So distinct is the realm of faith from the realm of empirical reality that to maintain that Easter asserts something about a body, that "facts" about a body are even included in Easter faith, actually "endangers" our understanding of Easter.[13] Strange as it may seem, we are here told that in the case of Easter empirical reality can only *endanger* faith, not reinforce it. The body in which Jesus appeared to his disciples after his resurrection is said not to be his historical body, for the postresurrection body enabled him to be unrecognized by them for a time. It bore some traces of his previous life: there were marks of the crucifixion, but in other ways it was different. Because of the difference between the earthly and the "risen body," the secularist concludes that the disciples never intended to assert a physical resurrection of the earthly body.

The two inseparable and essential elements of the Christian faith are: "the freedom which has become contagious is that of the historical Jesus, and the freedom of Jesus is that freedom which became contagious."[14] These points are summarized by the blik, "Jesus is Lord." A Christian is one who has been "grasped" and "held," "taken" by the piece of history which is Jesus. Such terms as "grasped," "held," and "taken" may appear to make a transcendent reference to God, but that is not actually the case: the transcendent-appearing element in Christian statements using such verbs only "indicates that something has happened to the believer, rather than that he has done something."[15] Every time a Christian is tempted to say that God did something to him, the secularist would have him translate the situation into meaningful terms by saying, "I experienced something that happened to me rather than doing anything myself." A feeling of passivity is the empirical synonym for "God's action."

The whole Nicene Creed can, and must, be translated into non-

[12] Cf. *ibid.*, p. 128.
[13] Cf. *ibid.*, n. 36.
[14] *Ibid.*, p. 166.
[15] *Ibid.*, p. 141.

transcendent terms referring only to Jesus and bliks. When that is done, reference to God the Father in the first article of the Creed is understood as a reference to the *oneness* of the Christian blik. After all, is it not true that the Father has traditionally represented the *oneness* of the Godhead? The second article of the Creed, which deals with Jesus anyway, states that the norm of the Christian blik is found in the historical person Jesus of Nazareth. The reference to the Holy Spirit in the third article of the Creed is really a reference to the fact that those who have the Christian blik always testify that it has grasped them. That understanding, too, is appropriate, for the Holy Spirit has traditionally been the agent of God's action in the world. Recognizing that we have been grasped by the blik is the recognition that grace has acted in us; we are not responsible for the gift we receive in Christ. The doctrine of the "essential Trinity"—that God is triune in himself not just in his external appearance to man—means, if anything, that we are dealing with a blik, an absolute perspective, not merely a provisional opinion.

Of course there must be changes in the understanding of prayer also. In appearance, prayer is obviously addressed to Another, but, since "God" is meaningless to a secularist, there is no one for him to address. Consequently the meaning of prayer must be looked for in terms of reflection and contemplation rather than in terms of personal presence and communion with God. Intercessory prayer then becomes reflection on a given situation in the light of the Christian blik which ends, wherever possible, with appropriate action. Where corrective or helpful action is impossible, the situation at issue must still be intensely contemplated under the influence of the blik, for personal freedom, even in the face of failure and disappointment, is an essential feature of that blik. Thanksgiving and adoration cannot be expressed to the Source of the universe for anything; instead, such activities are simply features of the secularist's own "joy and wonder" that he and the world (arbitrarily) exist and that he has been grasped by the blik that has grasped him.

Reviewing his effort at the secular translation of the Gospel, Dr. van Buren thinks that he has fulfilled Dietrich Bonhoeffer's goal of a religionless Christianity. "When Easter is in the center of the picture . . . we can then say that the meaning of the Gospel is to be found in the areas of the historical and the ethical, not in the metaphysical or the religious."[16] As we have seen, the secularist claims neither to speak of God analogically nor to use any circumlocution for "God." It is admitted that such key words as "free," "love," and "discernment" are not based on empirical experience precisely as such concepts as "undiluted," "gravitational attraction," and "sense data" are, but the former words are nevertheless empirically grounded. The only demand made of secularism if it is to be the fit vehicle of the Gospel is that it meaningfully employ a language which uses the first person singular pronoun.[17] That, as we shall try to show, is a most significant point, although its significance is not developed in the book we are examining.

When asked where the transcendent God of classical Christianity is and whether theology has not been reduced to ethics by its secular "translation," the answer given is: What more could there be for secular man? The only person not questioned in the whole presentation is secular man, the author's point of departure. The inability of much religious language to be verified in our sense experience should reduce the content of theology, but such a reduction, we are told, has been made in many fields to our advantage. Specifically, for example, astrology has been "reduced" to astronomy and alchemy to chemistry; in all such cases progress has been made because metaphysical pretentions have given way to historical fact.

Summarizing his case in traditional terms, Dr. van Buren asks, Does not God "reveal that he wants men to stop trying to peer into the clouds and to obey God's will by thinking out their existence in terms of man—specifically the man in whom God has said all that he has to say to men?"[18]

[16] *Ibid.*, p. 197.
[17] Cf. *ibid.*, pp. 170 f.
[18] *Ibid.*, p. 198.

I I I

Criticism of the Secular Gospel

Viewing the description of Christianity contained in the last chapter, we must admit that it addresses a vocal and vigorous group of contemporary men. In many cases good suggestions are offered for focusing Christianity in the world; the empirical hard-headedness and terminological simplicity of the presentation should appeal to many in our present cultural climate. But once we grant that there is an audience to whom such a presentation of Christianity may appeal, we must examine closely what the presentation says and the issues it raises. Does it translate the authentic Christian Gospel into terms meaningful today? The book upon which the preceding chapter was based is offered to men who are trying to be Christian, and the historical person Jesus of Nazareth is often referred to in it, but we may nevertheless ask whether or not the Jesus of Christian history can be adequately presented in the terms it allows.

There is common agreement nowadays that the old battle for the "historical Jesus" is over—or, more properly, that it was never able to be fought. The only Jesus we know is the one we see through the eyes of his disciples and through the life of the Church. That fact is not a drawback, however, for the essence of the Christian faith is that men can be incorporated into Christ, somehow sharing his Spirit and his mind. St. Paul wrote to the Corinthians that the deep things of God are folly to the natural man because they are spiritually discerned, but Christians need not despair for "we have the mind of Christ" (I Cor. 2:16). If

Jesus was the Son of God, he came to men in order to influence them; consequently there is no handicap in admitting that we know about him only through his influence upon others. Quite the contrary. If he did not or could not change others deeply enough to reveal him without distortion, he would not be worth bothering about. He would be an impotent fraud.

If Jesus did make a difference in men, that difference should show. To say that one aspect of the change Jesus wrought in his disciples was an increase in spiritual discernment would be the least one would expect considering the claims made for him. If such a change actually did occur in Jesus' followers (and we must give historical fact a chance to be itself), we must admit that his disciples had a better insight into who and what he was than people who were reacting against him in a close-minded, external manner. The "impartial witness" of nondisciples (or even of a contemporary secularist) under such circumstances could give us no significant insights into the true nature of the Jesus of history, for it would not be *witness* at all. It would be the projection of their views on to Jesus; quite a different thing. Realizing precisely that, contemporary scholars admit that if we want genuine, objective information about Jesus we must seek the Jesus of history only in *Christian* history, *in the witness of his disciples*.

C. H. Dodd has noted that the "problem of historicity" has shifted ground in recent years. The bare collection and recitation of historical facts did not precede the Christian Preaching or *kerygma*; instead, it was the other way around. "We are not to think of the record in the Gospels as the ultimate raw material, out of which the Preaching was constructed. The *kerygma* is primary, and it acted as a preservative of the tradition which conveyed the facts. The nearer we are in the Gospels to the stuff of the *kerygma*, the nearer we are to the fountain-head of tradition. There never existed a tradition formed by a dry historical interest in the facts as facts. From the beginning the facts were preserved in memory and tradition as elements in the Gospel which the Church proclaimed."[1]

[1] C. H. Dodd, *The Apostolic Preaching and Its Development* (New York: Harper & Row, 1960), p. 55.

As Christians we cannot want to know Jesus apart from the witness and testimony of those who responded to his call. Wanting to know about any man, we should go to his friends; we rightly prefer others to learn about us from our friends and we can best know Jesus through his friends. The Christian religion and its revelation are personal activities. When concern, sympathy, reciprocity, intimacy, and freely offered good will—conditions necessary for any truly personal activity—are absent, Christian revelation cannot be present. If one assents to the necessity for the personal conditions we have just mentioned, he has already agreed in principle that the Jesus of history cannot be separated from the Jesus of Christian tradition. Since the only Jesus we can significantly know is the Jesus of tradition, we must say in the beginning that if the tradition is wrong there is no significant Jesus left to know.

There are many times in the secular translation of the Gospel described in the last chapter when the reader wonders if the criticism of traditional Christian thought has not gone so far as to destroy any Christian significance to the remnants the secularist accepts. The Christian faith as traditionally practiced can at least partially be described in secular terms, but we wonder if that faith could have been lived in the first place, and can give anything more than the external appearance of being lived now, if the description we have reviewed is treated as Christianity's whole content. A chicken can run around a farmyard for a short time after its head is wrung off, but it does not last long. Once the momentum of Christianity has been built up through the ages, it can perhaps appear to continue even though some of its vital parts are missing, but that appearance will not last long. I cannot avoid the impression that the secular "translation" of the Gospel has done for Christianity what projecting a globe on a flat surface does for the globe. You can learn a lot of geography from a map, but in such knowledge a most important dimension of the actually existing world is missing. By taking one dimension away, what is left in the other dimensions is changed even though that is not one's intention.

I enthusiastically endorse the secular mind's healthy reaction against all transcendentalism that directs attention away from this world and that minimizes what goes on within the world. Christianity is a religion of redemption. The commendable motive behind the secular understanding of the Gospel is to make it impossible for Christianity *not* to redeem the world by saying there is nothing to Christianity but its action in the world. At least that is my impression. The position I shall try to present does not differ about the singleness of Christianity's role in the world; it differs in the understanding of the source of Christianity's force. I do not think that human action can be adequately motivated by anything less than a transcendental reference to God; I think man is less than himself if motives as mutually exclusive and arbitrary as "bliks" explain his behavior in the world. Bliks are not used by the secularist to explain the world, to be sure, but they are used to explain man's action in the world; even there, however, their lack of transcendent reference makes them inadequate for the whole man, as our later analysis of man will try to show.

The primacy of historical action in Christianity is an insight shared by the secularist and the position taken in this book. I shall contend, however, that a certain primacy of history extends to everything in the world in a manner which the secularist does not allow. To put the point in different words: although both positions stress the primacy of history, I shall contend that the secularist is not aware of all the constitutive elements of the history he endorses.

The secularist contends that we cannot argue about bliks; all we can do is describe them. A blik centering around Mary Baker Eddy is said to be as good as a blik centering around Buddha, which is no better or worse than a blik centering around Jesus. We cannot conclusively decide between bliks on empirical evidence according to the secularist, but we can tell empirically whether or not a person is living according to the blik to which he claims allegiance. We cannot empirically determine the truth or falsity of bliks, but we can empirically locate hypocrisy in professed adherence to a blik; for the secularist, then, hypocrisy, not error, is the only foe of the Gospel.

No Christian will want to deny that consistency is a virtue and that hypocrisy is evil; the problem is: Can genuine Christian commitment adequately be described in terms of consistency alone? Religious people claim to accept their religion because it is *true*, because it corresponds to reality. No doubt conflicting views of truth are claimed by people of different religious convictions, no doubt *the* truth is difficult and frequently impossible to settle by common agreement in these matters, but neither of these facts can justify the conclusion that truth is thereby an expendable dimension of religious living as the secularist maintains. Christian action can be *externally* described without raising the question of its truth or falsity, but as the religious life is lived from within, belief in its truth is its backbone.

Surely, as the secularist suggests, we are "caught" and "grasped" by certain views; that is one aspect of the religious situation, and an important aspect too. But it is not the whole story, for we must ask what grasps the religious believer. The first-person testimony of religious people is that, as we have indicated, they are grasped by the *truth*. To understand the situation in its entirety we must ask ourselves how the truth is discovered anywhere in our experience. It is never automatically recognized; a certain appreciation is necessary if it is to be known.[2] As people's appreciation varies, their ability to recognize truth varies, and thus the truth they recognize varies. Battles about "truth" are frequently disguised battles of appreciation. All the paintings in a gallery can be seen by anyone entering it and taking the trouble to look around, but, without the proper *appreciation*, a person will miss the paintings' true significance. Courses in musical appreciation are given—sometimes not very effectively—in our schools so that our children will be able to recognize the *true* meaning of musical communication.

Different religions in the world are to some extent "growing together" today because a oneness of truth is becoming apparent beneath varying appreciations of ultimate reality. A Hindu may have a better appreciation of the Christian doctrine of the Trinity than a nominal, nonpracticing Christian. Involvement and com-

---

[2] Cf. Austin Farrer, *Saving Belief* (London: Hodder & Stoughton, 1964), pp. 20 ff.

mitment in one's own religion are the best key to understanding another person's religion. That is an important insight which is beginning to affect the ecumenical movement: committed Protestants and Catholics understand each other and have more religious truth in common than insecure zealots have within each denomination.

Committed, inquiring people within one religious tradition find that they have insights and problems about their creaturely relation to God in common with religious people of other traditions. Appreciating common problems enables such people to appreciate a common truth that would scandalize their less appreciative— and therefore more dogmatic and provincial—fellow church members.

Appreciation determines what we can recognize as truth; it varies from individual to individual and from religion to religion, but even so appreciation does not substitute for the truth. Appreciation is an aid to recognition, not a replacement for what is recognized. Recognizing the role appreciation plays, however, it is quite possible for people to admit the discrepancy of appreciated truth from religion to religion without concluding from that discrepancy—as the secularist does—that religion does not deal with truth at all. The secularist conclusion follows only on a partial consideration of the situation.

No genuinely religious person denies the difficulty of determining the certainty of some religious doctrines in a manner acceptable to the experimental sciences, but he *should* deny that the concept of truth is exhausted by the limited operations of those sciences. The secularist allows a preconceived theory of truth to determine what Christianity must be; his approach to religion is one of antecedent legislation, not immediate and accurate description.

To reduce theology from truth-about-reality to consistent ethical action in the world, as the secular Gospel tries to do, and then ask what more there can be than a this-worldly ethic for secular man, is neither to have refuted the legitimacy of a transcendent God nor to have shown that secular man actually lives without important and necessary transcendent references. We will try to show a little further on that Dr. van Buren bases his whole hope for a secular Gospel on transcendence, but even if secular man does not admit the legitimacy of a transcendent God, that does not prove that the historical Jesus (in the only way we are able to know him, that is, through the Christian tradition) can be himself apart from such reference.

Only a God who is admitted to be something in himself can satisfy the Christian consciousness. To replace God by a "functional equivalent" such as "being grasped" or "feeling obligation" may do to fill out an abstract secular theory, but it will not sustain religious living in its fullness. Our consciousness is intentional; that is, its nature is to refer beyond itself and to ask questions about everything. If we can conceive the possibility of a legitimate question, we have, by that very fact, already conceived the possibility of a legitimate answer. My most immediate awareness of myself as a person is that I am entitatively more than a function. External, functional descriptions do not exhaust my being; I am more than just a consumer, husband, teacher, father, neighbor, voter, sports fan. Because I am more than a function my Christian consciousness will not allow God to be reduced to a function either. The awareness that we as selves transcend our external functions is the unshakable source of our asking questions about God until he is acknowledged to be "entitatively" existent in himself. Some kind of "entitative completeness" is what we attribute to God when we say he is personal.

When we are told that "the meaning of the Gospel is its use on the lips of those who proclaim it," we normally expect unbiased listening to be the first step in objective investigation.[3] We wonder if such listening is possible through secular ears. In the secularization of Christianity being presented to us, have people, past and present, who have lived according to the Gospel, really been heard? The mainstream of Christian history will charge that only lip service has been paid to the words on Christian lips. When that is the case, the investigator is cut off from the very data his axiom about listening claims to lay bare.

Men's presence in the world is the asking of questions of the world. Our very being is a quest for meaning, but in describing

[3] van Buren, *The Secular Meaning of the Gospel*, p. 155.

Christian freedom Dr. van Buren always separates its function from the experienced meaning of the person who is being described. Secular presuppositions prevent a consideration of the whole datum, furnished throughout Christian history, that the freedom men have caught from Christ has been possible for them only because it carries within itself a reference to a transcendent God. Because the data conflict with its preconceived categories, secular analysis is not empirical enough in its description of Christian freedom. It either omits the professed motivation of people who have caught Jesus' freedom or it rewrites the supposed motivation of Christians according to its secular canons. The evidence on the lips of those who have been grasped by Jesus' freedom is that they have been grasped *by God from beyond*. Their "being grasped" has a structure, and the structure is as immediate as the "grasping"; thus any talk of *their* being grasped without the structure *they* claim to perceive is not talk about their actual experience.

We have no evidence of Jesus' freedom apart from evidence that his freedom was based upon his life for God the Father! The freedom of Jesus was a God-oriented freedom. He was not just free; he was free for a reason, and that reason structured his life. Jesus was showing through his freedom that there is a Source of life beyond the world, obedience to which makes one free in the world. His freedom *is* reference to the Source beyond the world, to the Father.

Jesus was received by the first Christians (and by all Christians thereafter) as the unique revelation of the God of Israel. God chose the Israelites to be his special people (cf. Deut. 7:6 ff.), to be his Servant in the world (cf. Isa. 42, 49, 50, 52-53.); in Jesus the disciples recognized for the first time the true Servant who fulfilled Israel's vocation. Jesus was so completely recognized through the eyes of Jewish history and expectation that he was seen to be the embodiment and wellspring of a new Israel. His freedom cannot be separated from the vocation he was recognized to fulfill; we must constantly remember that he was received by those to whom we owe *all* of our knowledge of him (including his freedom) as the fulfillment of Jewish prophecy.

The importance of Jewish prophecy and Jewish expectation for the earliest Christian Preaching has been well summarized by C. H. Dodd: "The Pauline *kerygma* . . . is a proclamation of the facts of the death and resurrection of Christ in an eschatological setting which *gives significance to the facts*. They mark the transition from 'this evil Age' to the 'Age to Come.' The 'Age to Come' is the age of fulfillment. Hence the importance of the statement that Christ died and rose '*according to the Scriptures*.' Whatever events the Old Testament prophets may indicate as impending, these events are for them significant as elements in the coming of 'the Day of the Lord.' Thus the fulfillment of prophecy means that the Day of the Lord has dawned: the Age to Come has begun. The death and resurrection of Christ are the *crucial fulfillment of prophecy*. By virtue of them believers are already delivered out of this present evil age. The new age is here, of which Christ, again by virtue of His death and resurrection, is Lord. He will come to exercise His Lordship both as Judge and as Savior at the consummation of the Age."[4]

In the speeches of Peter in Acts, which seem to indicate "the *kerygma* of the Church at Jerusalem at an early period," the importance of previous expectation and fulfillment are also stressed.[5] In Acts 2:16 Peter says, ". . . but this is what was spoken by the prophet Joel. . . ." He also states, "But what God foretold by the mouth of all the prophets, that his Christ should suffer, he thus fulfilled" (Acts 3:18); and ". . . all the prophets who have spoken, from Samuel and those who came afterwards, also proclaimed these days" (Acts 3:24). There can be no separation of *tradition* and *Jesus' person* in Christianity. Just before his betrayal, the Gospel according to St. Luke reports Jesus as saying, "For I tell you that this scripture must be fulfilled in me, 'And he was reckoned with transgressors'; for what is written about me has its fulfilment" (22:37). After his resurrection Jesus is reported to have said, "These are my words which I spoke to you, while I was still with you, that everything written about me in the law of Moses and the prophets and the psalms must be fulfilled" (24:44).

Jesus' freedom was exercised and manifested in the context of a

[4] Dodd, *op. cit.*, p. 13. (Italics mine.)
[5] Cf. *ibid.*, p. 21.

long history—a tradition!—that was accepted as God's dealing with his chosen people. *The pre-existing meaning into which Jesus came as fulfillment structured his freedom and structured his disciples' recognition and experience of that freedom.* Expectation and fulfillment, cult and man, are so interdependent in the Gospel that we cannot isolate either pole from the other and remain true to the facts. To emphasize that *Jesus'* freedom has become contagious is to emphasize that we catch the very freedom Jesus exercised, but to catch his freedom we must also catch his meaning in exercising it and the meaning of the first witnesses who recognized it. To separate the meaning from the freedom is to make the latter less than personal. If Jesus' freedom becomes our freedom, then his meaning becomes our meaning, the structure of his life becomes the structure of our life, and we are able to be free in the world only because we recognize that our ultimate dependence is on the God of Abraham, Isaac, and Jacob—who so transcends the world that we cannot *properly* name him!

It is suggested that we catch Jesus' freedom in "discernment situations": what we discern is Jesus' freedom. But, as it stands, that suggestion is ambiguous. It must not be interpreted in a way that implies that Jesus' freedom appeared on the world scene *de novo,* as something striking in itself and which needed no reference beyond itself. To deny this is to theorize in the face of the evidence. To discern Jesus is to discern what he discerned; his freedom was itself intentional of something beyond it and cannot be itself apart from that reference. Jesus' freedom can be described in terms of his own prayer, "Father . . . not my will, but thine, be done" (Luke 22:42).

If we describe the practice of Christians in full and unbiased detail we must admit that they think they are referring to God in their religion. How they are may differ from how they think they are, but there is no doubt in their minds *that* they are. If we are going to adopt a functional analysis of religion, we must first let religion function for what *it* claims to be. Philosophical criticism is always reflective, that is to say, it always depends on something prior to it which furnishes it with its subject matter. Only because reality exists prior to and independently of reflection can we turn upon that reality in reflection; the primacy of reality's existence must be respected by all accurate investigation. Basic analysis should recognize the prior existence of its own principles; that is what any metaphysics worth its salt has always tried to do, and why the return to metaphysics would not do secular man the harm he thinks it would. We cannot deny, however, that such a return would harm many secular arguments!

Reflective analysis can show the structure of lived activity, but the primacy of our immediate relation to the world over our secondary acts of reflection prevents the latter from even gaining ultimate supremacy over the former. Lived reason gives reflective reason whatever value the latter has in our lives. Religion involves our *total* relation to reality; in such a relationship, *withdrawal* (reflection) can never replace *engagement* (life). That amounts to saying, as we will attempt to show in more detail later, that our primary encounter with reality always exceeds the formal nature of our expression. Reflective reason must be used to guide lived reason in its engagement with the world, but if the categories of reflective reason are allowed totally to limit lived reason in an a priori manner, the abstract will have conquered life, essence will have suppressed existence. To give a secular analysis of religion in categories that have been completely agreed upon before the analysis begins is to fall precisely into that error. The legitimacy of religion comes from a total engagement of man which precedes and transcends—although always involving—the formal use of words; an analysis of the words used in religion can reveal something of religion's structure, but it cannot finally deny religion's validity for it cannot circumscribe the spiritual source of man's religious activity.

The singularly significant remark in Dr. van Buren's exposition from our point of view is his assertion that if the language of secularism is to be sufficient for the Christian message it must be able to contain and use the first person singular pronoun. We are told that when a man says "I'm I" he is giving a "final explanation of himself and of his actions."[6] In another place the statement "I'm I" is said to have a *finality* about it and reference is

[6] van Buren, *op. cit.*, p. 168.

made to Ian Ramsey, from whom the author seems to have taken this point.[7]

Professor Ramsey, however, uses the phrase "I'm I" in order to add a dimension of reference to the more limited ones Dr. van Buren allows in his study.[8] Professor Ramsey claims that there can be neither the practice of religion nor the discipline of theology if self-awareness is not more than spatio-temporal objectivity and body awareness. When a person is persistently asked to explain some action of his life, such as his desire to fish, and he finally replies, "I do it because I'm I," Ramsey says that that person is giving the ultimate explanation of his behavior. To be a person is to have some ultimate autonomy over oneself, no matter how small it may appear from the outside. Since there can be no person without freedom, all truly personal living is decisive living, that is, the expression of a person's autonomy in decisions that are final for him just because they indicate what finally constitutes him as a person.

Dr. Viktor E. Frankl, a psychiatrist who was confined in both the Auschwitz and Dachau Concentration Camps in Germany during World War II, has written of his experiences in those camps and described what happens to people in such circumstances. His findings agree completely with the view of personal freedom we have just expressed. The prisoners who were "doomed," Dr. Frankl discovered, were those who lost the incentive to make decisions that were significant for the future, those who did not use their freedom to transcend their present circumstances. Forced to live together like lower animals in a death camp where smoke from a chimney indicated that hundreds of human bodies had just been removed from the gas chamber and were being burned for easy disposal, it is not difficult to see how men could lose hope for the future and be reduced to a dazed minute-by-minute concern for animal existence. Sensitive personal survival was possible even under such dehumanized conditions, however, for those who used their personal autonomy where they could. A man who would

---

[7] Cf. *ibid.*, p. 154.

[8] Cf. Ian T. Ramsey, *Religious Language: an Empirical Placing of Theological Phrases* (New York: Macmillan Paperbacks, 1963), *passim*.

think of future reunion with his wife and family, a man who would resolve to respond to a guard or a fellow prisoner with calmness, a man who could lead some life of his own within himself, perhaps imagining that he was lecturing to an audience about life in a concentration camp, could survive. If a person could somewhere save his self-respect by using his power of self-determination, he was not lost.

We are fully ourselves only in the exercise of our freedom; wherever there are choices to be made, our freedom will somehow show itself in the way we make them. If we cannot choose the circumstances of our life, we can at least choose the way we will react to them, and that is a valid example of personal autonomy. Dr. Frankl concludes that "there is nothing conceivable which would so condition a man as to leave him without the slightest freedom. Therefore, a residue of freedom, however limited it may be is left to man in neurotic and even psychotic cases. Indeed, the innermost core of the patient's personality is not even touched by a psychosis."[9]

Because our personal decisions are really ours, they cannot be reduced to externally observable, objective, predetermining factors. As Professor Ramsey puts it: "Plainly 'I' is in part tractable in observational language—what 'I' refers to is not something entirely independent of our public behaviour. On the other hand, it can be argued, and all those who (like Hume himself) find Hume's 'object' theory of themselves inadequate will certainly argue that 'I' can never be exhausted by such language. So, if we wish to speak of everything which, for each of us, this 'I' refers to, we shall have to use phrases which—while beginning with and having some foothold in observational language—are somehow or other qualified to make it plain that their reference is in part beyond such language as well."[10]

The plain fact is that the use of the first person singular pronoun is based upon a type of transcendence we all experience in our personal lives. The "finality" of the statement "I'm I" is due

[9] Viktor E. Frankl, *Man's Search for Meaning: an Introduction to Logotherapy*, trans. by Ilse Lasch (Boston: Beacon Press, 1962), p. 135.
[10] Ramsey, *op. cit.*, p. 42.

to the fact that man transcends every situation he is in and cannot be totally identified with any set of determinate conditions. In some aspect of his being he is autonomous and independent of antecedent determinations. When the implications of the finality of the "I" are drawn out, we believe that Ramsey's remark that the "I" behaves in a logically similar way to "God" in traditional Christian living is correct. From this small hole in the secular dike, life-giving water is able to flow into soil parched by overexposure to limited, formal analysis.

Transcendence is not the arbitrary, unfounded monstrosity the secularist thinks it is. We are not totally bound to the immediate situation in which we find ourselves; that is why we are able to employ *signs* and *symbols* in our lives rather than just respond to *signals* as the lower animals do. A signal, following the usage of John A. Hutchison, functions completely within the immediately given environment; it sets off anticipatory responses in a manner that can be completely explained in biological terms. Signs and symbols, however, *refer* rather than merely point to objects, which is to say that they can indicate more than one thing at a time and can be used to recall the past as well as to anticipate the future, both of which are dimensions transcending sensual immediacy.

Many times reference is made in Dr. van Buren's book to the plurality of language-games. We should stop and ask ourselves how there is able to be such a plurality. Where does the plurality come from? These are questions not asked in the book, but the answers are not difficult to find. The plurality of language systems comes from a unique ability of man—from his ability to look at the world from different points of view and with different purposes. Only because we as persons can transcend a given point of view and adopt another, can there be different functional uses of words for analysts to investigate. How odd it is to adopt the results of linguistic analysis but to shut one's eyes to the source which furnishes that analysis with its differentiated subject matter!

Men are always located in a world; we are nothing apart from that location, but we can transcend our location to some extent from within it. That transcendence explains why we are able to question everything. Why is the world the way it is? Why am I the way I am? Why am I related to the world as I am? Why do bliks and empirical statements arise within one reality? Why is it necessary to live by bliks? Why is Jesus' freedom contagious? Why could Jesus' personal identity transcend death?

The movement of my life indicates that I *am* these questions, as well as many more. Where I discover complexity in reality I am led by something in my own nature to look for a transcending unity. To be told that I should not (or cannot) is to be told that I should not (or cannot) be myself. The persistence of the question "Why?" is not just a psychological phenomenon, for we can ask the question "Why?" about psychology itself. Why am I able to have the psychological manifestations I do have? By being able to ask "Why?" about psychology we show that we transcend it, too.

We experience dissatisfaction with the composite and limited. That dynamism within us which challenges us to question and go beyond everything we can produce and find in the world must have its source beyond us. If something within me questions *all* that I am, including my very being, it cannot be written off as a comforting projection of my being. It is not a means by which I find satisfaction in the world, for it challenges everything about me including my satisfaction. Rather, it would seem to indicate that my being is oriented toward something more than I am—and more than my world is. We are not bottles which can be capped by the positive sciences and told that we are full; we have produced the positive sciences and we can question their sufficiency.

We have seen that, in spite of his own protest, secular man does argue from analogy. To anticipate our final conclusion, we may, accordingly, suggest to him that as we can explain the plurality of language games by our personal transcendence of them, so God explains the plurality found within us and the world by his transcendence of us. There is no necessity to take a big (or small) step *from* the world to get to God; instead, all we need to discover is what is involved in our life in the world as we actually live it.

Adopting a cognitive approach to religious language does not require consent to the claim that it "tends to mark off a certain area of experience as 'religious,' and it argues for a religious way of knowing, in contrast to other (secular?) ways of knowing."[11] Religious knowledge does not involve marked off and restricted areas of cognition, rather it involves a *total way of knowing* which permeates all restricted, special types of knowing. God is the intention of the whole movement of our being, not of a restricted area of the world. Therefore religious awareness is empirical although not experimental. Religion always deals with totalities; it is the totality of our world and our experience of it that need religious explanation. We believe that if the secularist departs from the total lived experience of man, instead of from a limited analysis of men's formal expression in their language-games, the *final* value of the "I" he does recognize will mean much more to him and will enable him to give a fuller explication of the Gospel than has been done in the essay we have examined. It appears to us that the secular translation of the Gospel with which we have been furnished actually does a good deal less than it purports to do and tries to do a good deal more than needs to be done. We do not deny that there is much in the broad history of Christian thought that needs re-emphasis, rethinking, and retranslation, but we do deny that the Christian Gospel can be adequately stated in secular terms that antecedently prevent the Gospel from making its own claims about itself.

We in one sense *are* transcendence; we prove that fact conclusively by producing different "language-games." If we will recognize ourselves in our full entitative existence, we will recognize the validity of asking—and even validly answering—entitative (yes, metaphysical!) questions. The questions we ask about the plurality of language-games and the nature of reality as a whole are questions which take their origin in the transcendence that makes us persons. If we can have questions based on such transcendence (as we do), then we can have legitimate answers based on the same transcendence (which we will try to show).

The reduction of astrology to astronomy and alchemy to chemistry dispelled ignorance because the pertinent data in each case were considered for what they were. The reduction of theology to

[11] van Buren, *op. cit.*, p. 99.

ethics and of the transcendent God of Christianity to the "contagion" of Jesus' freedom, on the other hand, are not profitable, I suggest, just because they are not based on a consideration of all the relevant data. Whenever Dr. van Buren convincingly explains himself to the practicing Christian, he has to lapse into the use of traditional terms and drop the quotation marks from around the word "God." In doing that he is saying more to others than a secular man can conscientiously allow himself to say, but in being forced to proceed that way he may actually be communicating better than he himself realizes.

I V

Morals and Man in Crisis

THE CRISES of our time are numerous, and they all involve the use of power.

When the word "power" is mentioned today our thoughts are apt to turn immediately to atomic power, and there is no doubt that we find crises there. If man's problems are as big as his power, his problems are growing—and will continue to grow. One of our national magazines recently featured a commentary on world events entitled "The One Great Question." The article illustrated how one problem in power leads to another, for the column discussed how the recent change in political power in Russia might affect power relations between Russia and other nations, all of these questions being asked against the ever-present question of the use of atomic power. The United States and Russia have signed a nuclear test-ban treaty; Britian is for it, but France is not, and China has now become an atomic power. Authorities recognize that India is capable of developing such a bomb in the near future and so are Japan, Israel, Egypt, and Germany. What will happen if even the smallest nations have atomic power at their disposal? A minor misunderstanding may turn into a major mistake. What will happen if a nation, in its hurry to develop an atomic bomb, settles for a "cheap" one producing a large amount of radioactive fallout when it is tested? Crisis leads to crisis.

Even apart from the atomic bomb, international and national politics are known as "power politics." Young nations are struggling for independence and power throughout the world; federations of nations in Europe and in Asia are developing (or are at least being planned by some for the future); our present international peace is nothing but one crisis after another as major power blocs of nations stand each other off. There are even power crises within the power blocs that were formed to ward off crises. At the present writing we are in the midst of such a crisis about the multilateral force which the United States has offered to equip with atomic weapons within the North Atlantic Treaty Organization, to give but one example. On the other side of the world, the Southeast Asia Treaty Organization is trying to contain Asian communism, while Vietnam, Korea, Indonesia, and Formosa are focal points of power crises.

Economic power is another source of problems. It too has its international aspects, but the ordinary citizen is most conscious of it as it affects his own family. One of the newer factors in the economic picture in the United States is that teenagers are controlling greater amounts of the nation's purchasing power. Ever more advertising is directed toward this age group; it is an advertising man's dream, for he can make his appeal to an impressionable, clan-motivated, quick-acting audience. Inflation, pension and insurance payments, allowances, savings, budgets for necessities, and spending money for luxuries can all be described mathematically, but the sum of human problems they occasion cannot be calculated.

Social problems are frequently described in terms of clashes within the power structure of our society. At the same time that the magazine to which I earlier referred was describing "The One Great Question" facing us today as that of Russia and the atomic bomb, one of our daily newspapers was describing civil rights as our "hottest and most perplexing problem." The latter problem also has its international manifestations in South Africa, parts of Europe, South America, and Russia, in addition to the United States. In our country we are told that the crisis is no longer one of "race problems" but of "human problems." Citizens are urged to begin thinking of this crisis in human terms, for the issues of the battle are no longer in Congress and the courts; they have been thrown into our homes—where, of course, they originated in the

MORALS AND MAN IN CRISIS 49

first place. To have a problem thrown into our homes is not an encouraging thought, however. In March, 1963, thirty-eight people in their homes in the Borough of Queens, New York, heard Catherine Genovese, a young woman twenty-eight years old, scream for help and watched her be stabbed to death without going to her aid or even immediately notifying the police. They were afraid of becoming involved. People robbed at nine thirty in the evening on Fifth Avenue, passengers attacked in buses and subways in almost all of our major cities while other passengers sit idly by, are signs of our times. In our large cities we are aware of an "urban problem," a convenient name for a collection of problems involving education, economics, religion, politics, psychology, and so on.

Sex is another area in which we recognize a crisis today. This crisis is a power crisis; the power is described as masculine and feminine. No one doubts the strength and ubiquity of this power, but few seem to know how successfully to control it. The problem is found in teenagers and in parents; frequently it is a problem for teenagers because of their parents. What are the roles of husband and wife, beau and fiancée, brother and sister, boy and girl? Raw sex is taking an increasingly prominent place in our novels, movies, plays, and general advertising. The immediate appeal of sex is a power advertising agencies exploit but do not understand.

Persons are involved in all the problems we have described above and yet few of us would admit that our personal crises are exhausted by the types and kinds so far mentioned. Our personal crises have an intimacy about them that seems to set them apart from "social," national, and international problems. No matter how cosmopolitan we may claim to be, in our personal lives we tend to live "pretty close to home"; we have enough problems at home with ourselves without looking for trouble elsewhere. Conflicts between mother and father and the role children will play in the family are power crises. What to do with leisure time and in sickness and in old age are questions of power; even our weaknesses are problems of power, for they concern its absence. Our ability or inability to manage power shows in every aspect of our behavior: in our defensiveness, our offensiveness, our phobias, compulsions, obsessions, anxieties, threats, and fears. We have taken specific examples of power problems from today's world; tomorrow some of the names and locations we have mentioned will change, but the type of problem will remain constant.

Christianity is, at least by claim, a religion of power. It traditionally believes in an almighty God, Creator of heaven and earth, who shares his power with men through a new dispensation of grace instituted through his only-begotten Son, Jesus Christ. But to all outward appearances, Christianity has not seemed to help much in our present power crises; in fact, it frequently appears downright impotent, and that appearance has caused a crisis in Christianity itself. Why doesn't it help? We suggest that one reason is that men do not understand the nature and operation of human power. Their ignorance of themselves is a reason for their misunderstanding of religion.

To be is to act—to do something. Only nonbeing is totally impotent; to approach impotence is to approach nonbeing. As long as man exists his crises will be crises of power, for existence is power. To be aware of shortcomings in our actions and problems in our control of power is to become aware of shortcomings in our being and to have problems with the nature of our existence.

A typical illustration can again be drawn from a recent magazine article. Entitled "God on the Campus,"[1] this article reported that a survey of 35,000 graduates from 135 colleges showed that about 8 per cent of Catholics, 10 per cent of Protestants, and 13 per cent of Jews "abandoned religious faith entirely" in college. (There was, let it be noted, no way of determining from the poll the nature of the "faith" which was held before college—or whether it was worth keeping.) The statistics so far quoted are not very shocking, so the article hurried on to say that "it is the weakening of conviction, the watering down of devotion, which is taking place among far larger numbers of students." Relative per cents of 22, 30, and 60 were then given in the above categories for students who admitted being "either fairly or very non-religious in

[1] *This Week Magazine*, March 8, 1964.

practice." (The interpretation of the poll assumes that this change was for the worse, but again no information was supplied to justify that interpretation.)

The article quotes Philip E. Jacob, professor of political science at the University of Pennsylvania, as saying that "the vast majority of today's college students profess belief in God. But there is a 'ghostly quality' to their religion. It is divorced from present-day concerns, lacking in social responsibility."

We are further told that The Cornell University Values Study found students' religion to be secular in the sense of competing on an equal footing with, and finally losing out to, family-, work-, and leisure-centered activities. The "decline" of students is not just religious, however, for the article continues by pointing out that many young people have "what psychologist Erik Erikson calls a 'crisis of identity' during their college years. The result has been a shocking rise in suicides and mental breakdowns on our campuses."

Leaving the article at this point, we must maintain that if a person's religion is primarily noted for its "ghostly quality" it will precipitate "identity crises" rather than solve them. One thing of which we may be sure is that we are not ghosts.

A crisis of identity is not facing college students alone; it faces all men in our time. Perplexed people in all walks of life are seeking their true identity. The abundance of literature about fulfillment, peace, happiness, and success testifies to the felt need of people to discover who they are and why they are. The person who has no time for such questions because of compulsive work or play is, in his way, still testifying to the primacy of the questions in his life.

In I Timothy 1:15 St. Paul wrote: "The saying is sure and worthy of full acceptance, that Christ Jesus came into the world to save sinners." The love of God for man is explicitly conveyed in these words, but an additional truth about man is implicitly contained in them: the truth that man exists only in a world. Wherever man finds himself, he finds himself in a world; he is himself only in that world, and that world, on the other hand, is always a world for him. We are not just *in* relation to the world;

we *are* relation-to-the-world. Our personal being is not a self-contained whole within a completely independent context; our being as persons is a pattern-of-living-in-the-world, a way of organizing the world. Personal being is a principle of spatial and temporal organization. We project a pattern of living around us which largely determines how the world will affect us. An oversensitive person, for example, hears something in casual conversation that other people do not because he is anticipating something other people are not. He, in one sense, projects what he is able to hear. The mode of being-in-the-world which defines every man is a projection which antecedently determines what he can experience in and learn about the world in all areas of his life.

We exist because there is a world and the world exists because of us. That truth is not a conclusion to which we argue in a specialized way in one of the positive sciences; it is the womb within which our personal lives first exist and never outgrow. The truth implicit in St. Paul's words has been significantly called to the attention of modern man—whether some of our contemporaries resent it or not—by the German philosopher Martin Heidegger. No one begins his life in a vacuum; we are all born into a history which we did not choose and which went on before us. That history is one of man making his world, and, as a result of our birth, we enter into a certain world of men more immediately than anything else.

The truth we are now describing is in direct opposition to the starting point of Cartesian philosophizing. Investigation of the most immediate empirical data at our disposal shows that we are not isolated subjects who can profitably wonder how we make contact with a distant, external world. We come to know ourselves within a world that is already present to us; taken in our full personal existence, we never have a problem about how to get a world. In fact, our *self*-awareness arises in our younger years out of a slowly developing contrast between ourselves and the world whose presence makes the contrast possible. When we say that we exist because there is a world and the world exists because of us, we must be taken to mean that we know of no such thing as an isolated subject and an isolated object. Subject and world imply each other; that is why man's being is most adequately described nowadays as being-in-the-world. Our being in its own nature is a transcendence, a relation to the beyond—to the world.

In our most immediate lives, we experience no isolated subject we can project from nor any isolated world we can project into. The correlation of subject and object to which we are now referring is a radical one; it says that subject and world depend on each other. When the dependence of the world on man is emphasized in this radical way, however, some people believe that the reality of the world's existence has been denied. But that is not the case. It is sometimes thought that if subject and world are as interdependent as we have indicated, we would have to deny the fact that the earth and universe existed before man. The solution to this problem depends upon realizing the difference between the world as a scientific object and man's immediately lived world. No one in his right mind would deny that the earth existed before man; of course it did! But the *meaning of the earth*—even of its *prior* existence—is correlative to (that is, dependent upon the initiative, purposes, and culture of) man. The prior evolution of the world is a relevant fact only as *it* is an element of man's cultural world.

The basic correlation of subject and object describes the basic constitution of man's being as a person; as such, it is a "global fact," a fact within which all other facts about him are found. Being-in-the-world is the nature of man's personal being. Without it he cannot be himself; it is the condition upon which all of his specialized activities depend, whether they be psychological, physical, mathematical, or religious.

We are ourselves in a world. We have seen that being-in-the-world is the condition of our being human; now we must go on to examine in more detail the conditions of our being-in-the-world. Recalling the words of a once-popular song will help us.

Some years ago literate but lovelorn people were singing:

> I ain't got nobody, and
> Nobody cares for me.

Jokesters were quick to seize the possibility of the lyrics and to suggest that at least the first line of the song was a good description of a ghost. Although some songs are ghostwritten, we can be sure that most of the people who sang this song were not ghosts. The plaint of the song was not that the singer had no body; it was that even with a body he was lonely. He wanted somebody else.

When we use the term "nobody" in our everyday speech, the word means "no one," that is, "no person." No one living in our present world can deny the correctness of this usage. The only people we know have bodies; to lose one's body is to lose one's membership in this world. Without a body a person is no place. Since our world is a correlation of places, the loss of place is the most serious loss of status a person can sustain. As a matter of fact, it is an open question to many people whether a person can, indeed, sustain a total loss of place. The attitude we take toward death is the attitude we take toward the problem we are now describing. Fear of death shows how serious our loss of place is. The one thing about death of which we are sure is that it destroys the body—that through which we have location in the world.

When we use the word "nobody" as a noun (so far we have been considering it as a pronoun), the dictionary tells us that the word means "a person of no influence, importance, social standing, etc."

Here again we may notice that the meaning of the word relates to our physical body in a most direct and literal sense. Our exercise and display of influence, importance, and social standing always proceed through the body. Our influence in the world proceeds through our bodies because, as we have just seen, we are in the world only in our bodies. How could the phrase "*high* and mighty" arise without a physical orientation to reality? The word "standing" in "social standing" refers to the body so obviously that it hardly need emphasis. In our age of ease it is perhaps worth noting that the real reward of social standing is social sitting. The order in which guests are seated around a table is one of the oldest status symbols in human history. But sitting as well as standing is possible only for a person with a body. When we talk about the way abstract points "stand" in relation to one another or speak of the mind as the "seat of knowledge" in a person, our obligation to the body is also apparent.

If importance doesn't show physically, the self-styled "man of the world" doesn't want it. His world—and the world of every one of us—is *first* defined by its physical characteristics and locations. The difference between materialists and theists does not show so much in their first definitions of the world as it does in their final ones.

We all find ourselves located in some specific place and time in the world through our bodies, but the specificity and confinement of such location is frequently one of the most annoying features of our existence. We don't want to be here; we want to be there. We don't want to live now; we want to live then. We don't like to miss anything. As we actually exist, however, we can only be where we are when we are: every day we wake up in, and come home to, the same house and family in the same neighborhood, facing the same decisions and struggling with the same problems.

In our scientific activities we can often get the "big picture" of physical reality. As a result, we are sometimes tempted to feel as expansive as our theories. But we should remember that our scientific theories serve their purpose only to the extent that the personality and peculiarities of the scientist who invents them do not enter into his calculations. The objectivity and success of science are based on its impersonal methodology. "Scientific truth" is something everyone must be able to understand and verify in exactly the same way under exactly the same circumstances.

Scientific verification depends, above all else, upon the repeatability of crucial experiments. The way such repeatability is obtained is by leaving out of the experiment the full nature of the person who performs it; nothing is more disruptive of objective scientific success than the human variable. That statement means, as we indicated in the first chapter, that man is successful as a scientist only to the extent that he is willing to deny some aspect of his personal identity in his scientific pursuits. The denial of which we are speaking is not always evident at the level of words; thus it will be helpful to illustrate our point with several specific examples.

When science employs the concept "space," it is not the kind of space in which we live our daily lives. *Our* space has a concreteness about it which always makes it a definite *place*. Such space radiates outward, as it were, from our bodies; we have no choice about where its center is. It always centers around us in our bodies, for *we* are spatial through our bodies. Even though I know the planets of our solar system revolve around the sun, to me as a person the sun is always "out there." In my personal life I am a center of space and the whole universe is located for me relatively to my body. The undifferentiated continuum of scientific space is completely foreign to the locations I experience in my daily living. To us as persons every point in space is *not* the same as every other; we prove this every time we feel offended when someone treats us as if "we weren't there." Because I am here, *here* is a special place for me and always will be as long as I live.

Scientific time is also different from personal, or historical, time. As William G. Pollard puts it: "Scientific time is the kind of time measured by a clock. It has extension and can be marked off in seconds, hours, and years. Historical time has no extension and cannot be measured. It can only be lived. It is made up of three domains—past, present, and future—each of which is different and possesses its own distinctive character.

". . . scientific time has no past, present, or future inherent in itself. If the solution of any scientific problem is plotted against time, the point representing the present moment must be marked on it as an arbitrary act imposed upon the solution from other considerations which are not a part of the problem itself. Once this has been done we *interpret* all parts of the graph to the left of this mark as past states of the system which the graph represents and all of it to the right of this mark as future states."[2]

In our personal lives, on the other hand, we have no choice about where the future begins or how much of our lives up to now must be considered in our past; we are identified with the present to such an extent that it cannot be where we are not and it must be where we are.

My "existential space," the space in which I live, is rooted in my body. The body installs me in being, and coenesthesis, the feeling of my body, is the constant setting of all my conscious acts.

[2] William G. Pollard, *Chance and Providence* (New York: Charles Scribner's Sons, 1958), pp. 98 f.

Gabriel Marcel has shown that our bodily existence, ourselves as incarnate, is the only true beginning for our self-knowledge. It is through the body that man is inserted into the world, and the world is always some kind of extension of his body. The body, then, is an "existence-type": "The world *exists* in the measure in which I have relations with it which are of the same type as my relations with my own body. . . ."[3]

I am in the world through my body, and it is through *his* body that another person enters my world. It is in our embodiment that we are accessible to one another, and that accessibility is immediate—although always incomplete. I am more than my body, but I am my body too. The body is not an object, an insight Maurice Merleau-Ponty joins with Marcel in underscoring. We are not behind our bodies; we are through them. Merleau-Ponty speaks of the body as one aspect of man's subjectivity; in his view, my body is a body-subject, rather than a mere object. Certainly the body is not an object in the usual sense of the word, for it is not detachable from us. We cannot step outside of our bodies and examine them from all possible sides as we can a material object. I am my body in a way which prevents me from being completely detached from it in my consideration of it. I am always in it looking out, even when I see myself in a mirror. I may refer to the members of my body, my hand or my foot, my nose, my eyes, as things I *have*, but these members are more than something I have—they are also *me*. That is why I exist in my outward behavior, not just behind it. We see a person's sorrow in his face, his laughter in his eyes, his defeat in his slump.

Since I am my body, my being is somehow extended; my life is necessarily involved in the spatial world. My orientation in being is through the material world; unlocated spirituality and inward-looking self-concern are foreign to my being. "I am not consciousness of my consciousness, locked up in myself, isolated from my body, from the world, and from the other. Through *my* body I am in the world, which appears to be our world and, therefore, my existing is an existing-to-gether, a co-existence. The philosophy of

3 Gabriel Marcel, *Metaphysical Journey*, trans. by Bernard Wall (Chicago: Henry Regnery Co., 1952), p. 269.

'I think' has to be replaced by that of 'we exist.' "[4] Through our bodies we are always located in a community and in the world; location is a primary feature of our being and we can try to deny it only at our peril.

Embodiment and the consequences of world and community membership which follow from it must not be thought of as events which once happened to us; they are more basic than that—they *are* us. "My embodiment is not an event that occurred at a definite moment. It must not be explained as if God 'infused' my soul into a body. Rather, my incarnation consists in this that I as spirit have been created in a transcendental relation to a situation in the material cosmos which demands a soul, and it is in this that consists the creation of the individual soul. Embodiment, therefore, is not an historical fact; it is a mode of being which, as long as I live, I do not cease to realize. I can obtain my ontological fullness only as an ego which *embodies itself continually.*"[5]

We began this chapter describing the crises of our day in terms of power. Difficulties in the use of power are the source of our problems, and the realization of our problems is itself powerful enough to overwhelm many of us. In what we commonly identify as both our religious and nonreligious problems, power looms before us; it is tremendous but foreign. Its strangeness is what defeats us. There it is—we cannot deny its presence—but we know neither how to approach it (for example, in the atomic and international problems of the world) nor how to use it (think, for example, of the power God offers man in Christ). Power suddenly appears before us, but we feel isolated from it and consequently helpless in its presence.

As we sometimes "fight fire with fire," some people think all we need to do in our present difficulties is externally to oppose power with power. People who see victory over the problems confronting us simply in terms of a guaranteed annual wage, a minimum (or maximum) work week, an international police force, a larger

---

[4] William A. Luijpen, O.S.A., Ph.D., *Existential Phenomenology* (Pittsburgh: Duquesne University Press, 1960), p. 191.

[5] Stephan Strasser, Ph.D., *The Soul in Metaphysical and Empirical Psychology* (Pittsburgh: Duquesne University Press, 1957), p. 148.

domestic police force, more power in government, more benefits to the sick and aged, and so forth, are of this type. All of the suggestions we have just listed, and many others like them, are attempts to control the personal problems of men in society by bringing some external power to bear upon them. "Let power do it!" But power alone cannot do anything; we need directed power, power that is understood from the inside. But how do we understand it? Simply to oppose the power of lawlessness with the power of police is to trap people in a power squeeze. It is a suggestion that a majority who does not want to be disturbed makes to itself in order to control a minority who is disturbed; it is an attempt to regulate people from the outside instead of actually helping them in their lives.

People are caught in a power squeeze today; we cannot avoid it. The power we have for mass production requires that it be answered by the power of mass consumption. Mass markets, on the other hand, require mass tastes; thus man as a singular person tends to be minimized if not obliterated. The laws of large numbers so rule our lives that we dare not be ourselves. The expectations of others, not in a personal sense but in an economic or political sense, bear heavily upon us. Such personal virtues as thrift, temperance, purity, almsgiving, and integrity are now unexpected in society if not actually denounced. We are told we must buy in order to maintain a healthy economy; temperance is a concern only if drunkenness interferes in our relations with others; purity obviously will interfere with our relations with others, thus it is no longer desired; almsgiving is regulated by how much we can gain through income tax deductions; personal integrity is something we must be prepared to sacrifice if we want to get ahead in business. Because we view the checks and balances of power in terms of large numbers in a mass society, the value of personally motivated self-discipline is not only lost but no longer thought necessary.

Our inability to handle the crises that confront us and the danger of living under the conditions we have just described will be better understood if we ask how we are introduced to power in the first place. We should not be surprised to discover that our first introduction to power is through the body, the way we are introduced to being. In the beginning of our lives our world is obviously one of action rather than one of contemplation. The life-world of the toddler, for example, is shown in his play pattern, the style of his life at that time. He likes to explore and exert himself, as any weary young mother can testify. The toddler's world is one of carrying, swinging, jumping, lifting, and pushing. Our first concerns about infants are when they hold their heads up, when they will reach for daddy's little finger, when they will roll over in their cribs and begin to sit upright. As they grow older, boys and girls test their power in games, which accounts for their consuming interest in sports. They belong in their world by racing one another, performing stunts, playing baseball and football, and daring one another to do what they can do. After a while girls cannot keep up with boys where brute strength is required, but they frequently find compensation for this through the power of words—an excellence which sometimes leaves even an older man dumfounded!

The primacy of our orientation to reality through the body has recently been shown by studies made of children who are poor readers. It was found that children with poor physical co-ordination often have trouble reading; improving their co-ordination and orientation of space helps their reading. The remedial reading room in many of our grammar schools now looks more like a gymnasium than an academic classroom; it contains balancing boards of various types, juggling balls, and beanbags. Drills and exercises are held to improve balance and awareness of the multiple perspectives of things around the student. No one remedial method works for all children, but generally speaking, the more of a child's physical being that is involved in his reading the quicker he learns to read. Some children are helped by writing in large script on chalkboards, others must see, hear, say, and write words in order to learn them. Caleb Gattengo of London has devised a color system to teach the sounds of vowels and consonants; each of the twenty vowel sounds and twenty-seven consonant sounds of English have a special color. This system gives an added dimension by which the pupil can learn to associate sounds with the images used in writing.

Corroborating evidence has also been found on work done with brain-injured children. Words, reading, and talking—marks of the human world—seem to "grow out of" a primary, physically active involvement in the world. The progression from crawling to creeping to walking to talking gives evidence of not being arbitrary. Children whose development has been retarded by brain injury have made noteworthy improvement in many instances through having their limbs manipulated in "patterning movements" devised to reproduce the pattern of movements ordinarily controlled by reflexes in the brain. After several years observation, over 85 per cent of one group had made progress; 59 per cent began to talk for the first time; some acquired a vocabulary and others began to read at ages younger than would be normally expected.

Our bodies locate our first introduction to power; our lives in our bodies are our intimate lives, thus we may ask what is happening in our most intimate use of power today. The answer is found in elevators, escalators, automobiles, remote control TV tuners, all sorts of automatic devices for convenient living, the location of cabinets that makes stooping unnecessary, knives and toothbrushes that move themselves, carts with which to ride around golf courses, and an infinite variety of mechanized production techniques.

The robust person is no longer the privileged person. By means of our heating, air conditioning, and lighting systems all men are protected from natural uncertainties; *isolation from risk* is the goal—and increasingly the product—of our civilization. The primary risk of modern man, adopting a description made by Georges Gusdorf, is that of becoming more and more fragile. New medical techniques are being made available to all people. Immunization programs can be carried out for the total population of a country. Professor Gusdorf describes the human body as a closed battlefield where germs and antibiotics battle in a way which makes the person less and less the author of his health. What is more fragile, he asks, than a "grand champion"? Such a champion's power is narrowly defined, the result of overprotection and an extreme dependence upon an artificial environment. In our own country we find that what were once known as "participating sports" are increasingly becoming "spectator sports"; we identify ourselves with a golfer, tennis player, or football player and find his physical power sufficient gratification for our felt needs. Professional athletes grow rich as we grow soft.

We use furniture so soft that our doctors make us sleep on boards; we have food so rich that it must be kept from us if we are to keep our teeth; we have bodies so weak that therapeutic strenuous exercise is our only alternative to chronic aches or acute heart trouble.

Failing so miserably in his primary acquaintance with power in his body, is it any wonder man feels insecure and helpless in the face of the political, social, and economic power he must confront in the world? "It is only when contemporary man has again become master of himself that he will be able to believe himself truly master and possessor of the universe. For the moment, defeated by his conquests, he can only doubt concerning the world and himself, and compensate for this doubt by despair, or the frenzies of fanaticism. The virtue of power, preliminary condition of a return to order, is the foundation of all wisdom possible as the resolute affirmation of man in the world."[6]

[6] Georges Gusdorf, *La vertu de force* (Paris: Presses Universitaires de France, 1960), p. 12.

V

Man's Action in the World

WE HAVE seen that man is always located in a world and that he must exercise his power in a world. There is more to it than that, however, for to be a person in a world *is* to exercise power in that world: being in a world and exercising power are not a permissive conjunction; they are a necessary identity. We are never totally passive in our worlds. Thus our worlds cannot adequately be viewed as mere assemblages of situations; they are also assemblages of *tasks*. When we think of the situations in which we find ourselves, we are considering ourselves in our passivity, as we are limited by factors surrounding us; when we think of the tasks we must perform, we are considering ourselves in the active aspects of our being which enable us to be responsible persons.

Man is unique in the animal kingdom, we have also seen, because he is the animal least satisfied with the world as he finds it and because he cannot be completely defined in terms of what is given to him from external sources. He is the animal who most completely makes his environment. Rats do not make their own mazes and mice do not make their own traps, but man makes the cities in which he runs around like a maze and we saw in the last chapter how he can trap himself by his own accomplishments. Millions of people know nothing but a man-made environment; everything around them is there because of the prior activities of men. From the time they are born in a man-made hospital until the time their bodies are laid in man-made caskets or burned in man-made furnaces, people walk on streets or floors which are man-made; they hear nothing but man-made sounds—brakes, sirens, music, arguments; they eat only what man has prepared; they breathe what man has cooled, conditioned, or contaminated; and they have eyes only for what man most strikingly illuminates in neon.

Why has the life we have just described come about? Because man cannot be himself by accepting things as they are. A person is a center of activity who is defined by his activity. To be a person is not just to accept; it is actively to question. A person accepts only while questioning. To question is to challenge; thus we receive information from the world around us only in the context of a determining activity proceeding from us. We cannot be described in terms of reaction alone, as behavioristic psychology attempts to do. We cannot be completely defined in terms of our situations because we play an active part in determining our situations. A person can never adequately be studied by tests performed upon him in a laboratory; by submitting him to laboratory conditions he is removed from the context within which his whole being can manifest itself. By viewing him only as a reactor in our laboratories we artificially remove him from the world in which he is his full self as a person. If we make experiments upon people designed only to test their objective reactions, we should not be surprised at never discovering their reality-as-subjects.

The biggest lesson the human sciences have to learn today is that if they are to be themselves they must quit seeking the type of clarity found in the positivistic sciences. Clarity is obtainable only by abstraction and reduction. To think clearly about some subject matter we must abstract it from complicating factors that accompany it in the actual world and reduce our attention to a narrow field. Man is himself, however, only in his concrete relations with a concrete world. To abstract from the totality of his relation to the world is to abstract from him, and thus not to know him as he actually exists.

We most properly exist as persons with other persons. As a matter of fact, although clarity is what we seek in knowledge, clarity—at least of the mathematical kind—is what we least understand. Nothing is more foreign to us as persons than the notion of mathematical simplicity. A mathematical unit is simple, but we do not experientially understand what such simplicity is like. When I am trying to explain my relationship to another person whom I love, I have a great deal of difficulty putting it in "simple terms," but I understand what it is to have loving dialogue with another person better than I understand what it is to be a mathematical unit! We know other people better than we know the objects in our world, for we know the objects in our world only through other people.

Some insight into the primacy of persons to things in our lives can be gained from observations made on children. Babies who have been separated from their mothers, but who have been given good physical care, deviate very quickly from normal development. Deprived of personal contact with their mother (or another human substitute), babies lapse, within a few days, into a state of "silent grief." After a few months of such human isolation they develop the behavior patterns of adult psychotics. If the mother returns within three or four months, the child recovers; if the separation continues, the whole development of the child is retarded. His linguistic progress lags, if it is not completly destroyed, and his resistance to infection is also lowered, making him an easy victim of even the mildest diseases. There is no substitute for the whole presence of one person to another. Our "intuitive," because *immediate*, awareness of another person can never be reduced to something more elementary than it, for it alone enables us to develop completely enough as persons to make the mistakes we can make about it in behavioristic psychology!

Ludwig Binswanger has admirably stated the matter: "In every psychology that makes man, as such, into an object—particularly those psychologies founded by natural scientists such as Freud, Bleuler, von Monakow, Pavlov—we find a rift, a gap through which it is clear that what is being scientifically studied is not the whole man, not human-being as a whole. Everywhere we find something that overflows and bursts the bounds of such a psychology. (This 'something,' which is not given even a passing glance by natural-scientific psychology, is precisely what, in the eyes of anthropology, is most essential.) Limiting ourselves to Freud, we need only open one of his works at random to come upon this 'something.' We see him, for example, writing of the construction and operation of *our* psychic apparatus, of *our* psyche as that precious instrument by means of which we maintain our lives; we see him writing about *our* psychic life, *our* thoughts.

"With all these *possessive pronouns*, what is being spoken of is a being that is presupposed as self-evident and that is just as self-evidently being bracketed out, namely, *existence as ours.* The same is true, of course, of the *personal pronouns* in such phrases as: 'I think, I am inclined, he declares, he reports, he recalls, he forgot, he resists, I ask him, he replies, we establish, we trust the future, we were agreed,' etc. Here, too, what is being spoken of is an existence as *mine, his,* and so forth, and an existential communication, an interhuman or we-relationship, a relationship, that is, between a person and someone *like him,* namely, another person. When this *my* or *our,* the *I* or *he* or *we* are bracketed out, the result is that psychology becomes 'impersonal' and 'objective,' while losing, at the same time, the scientific character of a genuine psychology and becoming, instead, natural science."[1]

There is an essential spontaneity to human existence; man is a positive activity in himself before he is a reaction to his environment. The world of the "we" to which Binswanger refers is a manifestation of ourselves which both precedes and escapes any analysis which tries to treat man as if he were only a reacting object. Man's essential activity in the world can be described in terms of the temporality of his being; his temporality—his historicity—always includes, as we have seen, the modes of past, present, and future. He is never just a past, just a present, or just a future. A person is a present which contains a past and points toward a future. Again we must understand that man does not *have* a past, present, and future as properties that are distinct from him; he *is* past, present, and future. The temporality of man's being to which we are referring enables him to escape—at least to some extent—the immediacy of every situation in which he finds himself; that is why he cannot be described completely

[1] Ludwig Binswanger, *Being-in-the-World: Selected Papers translated and with a Critical Introduction to His Existential Psychoanalysis* by Jacob Needleman (New York: Basic Books, Inc., 1963), p. 169.

in terms of his situation. As long as he is himself, he transcends every present situation toward the future; a part of his
being is necessarily ahead of himself. Man's present is a presence
opened toward both the past and the future. Because he transcends every situation toward the future, that is, because he can
see the possibility of making new situations, he has a certain
responsibility for the world found in no other animal. Man recognizes different possibilities in the present; his being in the present
is a project toward the future. Because the temporal nature of his
being requires that he be a project toward the future, his being
cannot be a mere datum, a mere given, in the world; he cannot be
completely defined in terms of past, external forces.

The primacy of the human dynamism we are now describing is
of the utmost importance. Our being-in-the-world is active and
our activity gives meaning to the world. The project or task of our
lives is to humanize the world, which is only another way of
saying the same thing. We humanize the world—make it fit for
man—by giving our meaning to it. Because our being as persons is
active, that being is essentially expressive. Professor James M.
Edie writes: "Man is expressive even before he speaks: in his
corporeal attitudes, in behavior, in gestures, in rhythmic movements and tonal utterances, in the creation of artifacts, works of
art, and social institutions of all kinds. Man is expressive by his
very existence; as Merleau-Ponty observes, for instance, a man's
face is condemned to express *something* even in sleep, even in
death. Speech is but one form, doubtless a late and derived form,
of expression, and persons who have lost the ability to speak have
not for all that lost the ability to express themselves. The schizophrenic all rolled up in a ball with his face in his hands and unable
to utter a sound is still 'speaking' in the only way he can. In fact
he shouts. Or, to take another example, most friendships are inar-
ticulate. Authentic kindness and sympathy for another are seldom
'spoken about'; they are simply *done* and *accepted* on a level of
sub-understood, implicit, mutual comprehension which *is* the
more *expressive* the less is 'said' about it. No man can rely on
language alone to say what he *means*."[2]

[2] James M. Edie, "Expression and Metaphor," *Philosophy and Phenomenological Research*, XXIII, 4 (June, 1963), p. 539.

We do not enter the world as "empty tablets" waiting for reality to inscribe its secrets in us before we are able to express ourselves. We are not just "bare minds" waiting for nature to impress us for what it is in itself, nor are we sponges passively waiting to absorb whatever comes our way. Our relation to reality is more dynamic than anything suggested in the previous analogies.

Our being is not self-contained and complete in itself. As we have seen, we are not free to enter or not to enter into relation with the world. We *are* questions put to the world. The bundles of biological, sensual, emotional, volitional, and cognitive tendencies which modern science has enabled us to know ourselves to be must be understood as so many types of questions we ask of reality simply by being present to it. All of these questions are ways we consciously or unconsciously express ourselves.

My body, for example, is not a mute, isolated entity self-sufficient and self-contained. We have seen that it is in one sense *I*, and through it I as a subject am constantly asking questions of the utmost importance. My body's merest presence *anywhere* is the asking for the kind of world that can give me physical support and sustenance. The solid earth, chairs, beds, and sidewalks are different kinds of affirmative answers from the world to some of the questions which *are* my body's presence. The personnel manager of a business concern, worn out by a day of arbitrating personal problems, who wearily drops into bed at night and feels its support under his relaxing body, is carrying on dialogue with the world through his body and discovering satisfying meaning in that dialogue.

Similar dialogue is found in the behavior of the young boy who is excited about his new tennis shoes. As soon as he can get them out of the box and on to his feet, he rushes outside, or more spontaneously dashes across the living room, to see how fast he can run and how quickly he can stop in them. He and his world are communicating through his activity. The small child standing in the puddle and letting mud ooze up between his toes experiences an answer to a question he is asking of the world through his toes. The businessman who digs his cleats into the golf course on Thursday afternoon or pounds his desk on Thursday morning when he thinks that an unexpected appointment may cause him to miss his golfing date is also carrying on an expressive dialogue with the world. A girl on a dance floor is asking as many questions of the floor by dancing on it as her partner may be asking of her during the dance. All of these people experience anticipated, although little thought of, meaning as the world positively responds to the questions their bodies put to it.

On the other hand, a person who suddenly finds himself falling through empty space is frightened and shocked because of getting a "no" answer to the support his physical self anticipates and seeks. Even though a free fall through space may not be the answer he would hope for in his world, it is still an answer to one of the questions which is his body and thus is a significant part of his world. Such an experience supplies a basic meaning of the word "fall." From it many of our extended and derivative uses take their origin. We know how disastrous the fall of an empire or a point in an argument can be because we know how disastrous a fall can be to us.

As sentient and knowing persons our relation to the world has been compared to a light illuminating a surrounding darkness. Just as light enables objects to become visible by its rays, so our dynamic tendencies toward the world enable the world to respond to us in ways significant for us. The "light" which is our being, its anticipations and requirements, furnishes perspectives in which reality is meaningful to us. Sex is a good example. When a woman says "It is a man's world!" she means a man's world differs from hers—and the man's looks best at the moment. The worlds of men and women are not the same, for differences of sex constitute different modes in which we anticipate and project ourselves into the reality which surrounds us. The human world must be composed of two worlds, male and female.

The expression which is ourselves determines to a large extent what our world can be, for we, just by being ourselves—by *being* an active, "natural light"—determine what reality can say to us through our antecedent illumination of it. Our task is to "make meaning" out of the reality which exists beyond the horizon of our already-defined worlds. There is an indefinite extension of reality around us which is potentially meaningful to us but not yet actually meaningful; we give it meaning by projecting our "light" into it, thus enabling it to respond to our initiative in ways significant for us.

An obvious, but therefore good, example of the primacy of our activity for the meaning of the world can be shown in the world of the baby. Meaning in a baby's world is always behavioral and functional; his activities and interests determine what will be significant for him and what he will discriminate between. Babies are concerned with "action-objects." A staircase means nothing to a child who can only sit up, but it takes on a sometimes overwhelming meaning as soon as the child is able to walk and climb. The staircase then becomes significant to him because it is something he can climb. Our activities in the specialized sciences and in other areas of our life may be more subtle than a young child's, but they nevertheless give meaning to our worlds just as his activities do to his world.

Our first acquaintance with power and meaning is through our bodies; our first worlds are defined in terms of the obvious bodily actions we have illustrated from children: grasping, sucking, pushing, pulling, rolling, sitting, walking, playing. A milestone is reached, however, when a child learns to talk. Words are themselves a type of, or at least akin to, bodily gestures, for they are truly a means by which we *handle* reality. Through words we come to possess our world in a new way, and it is through words that we come to possess new worlds. Once children have learned to use words they want to know the name of everything. "The child frequently appears, in his naming mania, to be seeing the world for the first time, as though names were able to fix and stabilize his experience, and make it really his. It is almost as though the names had greater reality than the objects themselves, as though the objects took on a new existence when fitted into the peculiarly human and intimate framework of language. We see the same tendency at work in later development, where it is unpleasant or not nice to talk about certain things, as though by preserving silence one could prevent facts from existing."[3]

[3] L. Joseph Stone and Joseph Church, *Childhood and Adolescence: A Psychology of the Growing Person* (New York: Random House, 1957), p. 120.

Our parents, by teaching us the names of things, by scolding and praising us, are in effect enabling us to enter *their* world. We enter the domestic world of our parents and the world of their basic values in acquiring our first vocabulary. When we go off to school we enter new worlds through the words we learn there. We enter into the world of our state and nation, the world of science, politics, history, music, literature, philosophy, and religion in this way. But the meaning of a language always transcends its verbal expression, for, since we learn our language from others, the meaning of that language can never be considered apart from our initial we-community with others. The full meaning of any language refers beyond its formal expression to the intentional act of consciousness of the person who uses it and to the historical community within which the language is learned and understood.

As a result of what we have so far determined in this chapter we should now be able to understand how, for man, *meaning precedes explanation; commitment precedes withdrawal; action precedes reflection; the concrete precedes the abstract; apprehension precedes deduction; the correlation of I-we-world precedes theory.* There must be a meaning to our world before anything in it can be significant enough to require an explanation. We are committed to a world before we can step back from it to reflect upon it. Our concrete presence with others in a co-operative world is the context within which all of our theories develop; it is the beginning which none of them can contain.

We have made repeated references to the fact that man is himself only in a world; that in itself, however, is not the distinguishing feature of man, for it is true of all living beings, plant or animal. The special thing about man is *how* he is in the world. He is in it as transcending it. We have previously referred to man's transcendence, but Ludwig Binswanger has stated the matter so well that his statement has become "classical" within a few years of its appearance: "The animal has its environment by the grace of nature, not by the grace of freedom to transcend the situation. That means, it can neither design world nor open up world nor decide independently in and for a situation. It is, and always has been, in a once and for all determined 'situational circle.' On the other hand, the 'having' of a 'world' on the part of man implies that man, although he has not laid his own foundation himself but was thrown into being and, insofar as that, has an environment like the animal, still has the possibility of transcending this being of his, namely, of climbing above it in care and of swinging beyond it in love."[4]

The ability to "be beyond" is the distinguishing feature of man's being-in-the-world. It is only because we transcend our immediate situations that we can know things objectively. The word "object" is composed of the prefix "ob," meaning "before," and suffix "ject," meaning "to throw" or "put." Taken in its root sense, "object" means "to throw or put before," "to oppose." Understood in this way, objects do not exist apart from us, independently of us; they exist only as we enable them to be objects by the way we stand over against them. The world outside of us is something in itself, but what we know of it is always correlative to the approach we take to it.

Transcendence is not a faculty of our being; it is our being. Will, decision, conscience, freedom, are not faculties or specifically locatable functions of a self which underlies them. They are the posture of the whole person as a person in the world. Things have personal value for us because we are free, that is, not compelled, in obtaining them. Love, truth, beauty, virtue, and holiness cannot be themselves if we are not free to deny them. Knowledge, for example, is a creative act. If we are not free to say that something is false (or not true) when we say it is true, the very concept of truth is meaningless.

Since man's freedom is one with his being-in-the-world, his freedom is not absolute. It is always located and cannot be itself apart from that location and limitation. Such limitation, of course, is not a new discovery; it lies at the basis of the centuries-old practice in Christian moral counseling of discouraging people from making "heroic resolutions." A man is not free to become

---

[4] Ludwig Binswanger, "The Existential Analysis School of Thought," in *Existence: A New Dimension in Psychiatry and Psychology*, ed. by Rollo May, Ernest Angel, and Henri F. Ellinberger (New York: Basic Books, Inc., 1958), p. 198.

what he is not overnight. The pattern of living which is our being-in-the-world is too complex to be changed in an instant. Heroic lives are those lived with day-to-day consistency: those that show a consistent pattern of choice through ups and downs, changes and chances. One's character is not changed in a day, although the motivation for such change may suddenly command, or at least refuse completely to retreat from, our conscious attention. Isn't that, in fact, exactly what happens when we say that our conscience "haunts us"?

Personal power is transcending power—the constant going beyond the formal, the immediate, the past, and the present. Our very presence in the world gives a type of meaning to the world, but that meaning is the beginning, not the end, of our lives. Once reality is significant and important to us, our task is constantly to give that reality *new* meaning as we more fully manifest ourselves in it. The meaning we give to the world in our use of it is the way we can be said to make our world, and, because of our essential dynamism, our world always needs making.

Our task as persons is not to let "nature" have the last word. Once we have asked nature questions through our daily lives and our scientific activities, we must accept her answers first of all for what they are. Acceptance is necessary for a healthy life. If, through chemical tests, we ask whether or not a certain mineral specimen is gold and the answer is "no," we must accept the fact. But no matter what answer nature does give to man, he has the power, once the answer is accepted, to give new meaning and value to the answer by the use he makes of it. If nothing else, he can make a joke about "fool's gold." We all have to grow old—the attempt to look young must fail in the end—but there is such a thing as growing old creatively. A person who expresses himself through his age rather than letting his age express itself through him, is the man who knows what living is all about. The way a person ages is more significant than the fact that he ages; we are meant to give meaning to age.

Physical power, the power of an atomic explosion, is apt to impress us as the highest kind of power we know. Atomic power is the type that exists in our sun and which is found in unimaginable quantities throughout the staggering number of suns in the universe. But for all of its magnitude, force, and extension, such power is not the highest kind we know, for it is, so to speak, always power of the status quo. It is there, but once we understand that fact, it does not surprise us because it is always present in the same sense that it was present in the past. Physical power, although tremendous, is the lowest form of power because it is not creative. It can only be its already-known self. The power to do something new is a higher power than that which is limited by its own past. Physical power may make the biggest appearance at first sight, but truly human power does not rest in first appearances—it can grow through hindsight and even employ foresight.

A physically well-developed man or woman is pleasant to view. Such people are frequently used for models in advertisements because manufacturers want their products associated with "things as they should be." But it is possible to become too muscular and too preoccupied with physical culture; men and women who spend all of their time and attention on the development of their bodies end by disgusting us. Human power begins in the body and is located in the world through the body, but that power always transcends the body. Such power cannot be judged by appearances, for its very nature is to go beyond appearances. To let the external appearance of success be the criterion of one's success is to be the greatest failure of all as a person. The salesman who refuses to compromise his honesty to please his boss may not get the promotion that otherwise would have been his, but he has displayed his power in a time of crisis. The highest human power is virtuous power, power directed and controlled, creatively expressing the person. Personal power shapes the given; it does not rest in or aim at external rewards. Its fullest use is the confirmation of the self through the meaning it gives to the world.

Because our human power is necessarily found within a world, it is necessarily situated, as we have seen, within some factors beyond its control. Since we cannot control every aspect of every situation in which we find ourselves, acceptance of the possibility of immediate, external defeat is a necessary condition for the proper exercise of our power. A scientist does not expect every experiment to succeed, nor a composer every song to be popular. The important thing is that each person must express himself. Instead of being commended for his honesty a salesman may be penalized. Risk is involved in being human; cowards are less than human because they try to avoid risking their lives in their lives. Human power shows its strength precisely in taking risks; physical power cannot even recognize the challenge of a risk! The thinker who is afraid of ridicule and nonacceptance among his colleagues loses the chance to be as effective and powerful as he might be in human history—and he also loses the chance to be himself.

Our personal security, as our true personal success, must be found in the values we choose to actualize in the world rather than in an external appearance of success. Religious men have always distinguished the way things appear in the eyes of the world from the way they appear in the eyes of God; even the author of the Epistle to the Hebrews wrote: "As it is, we do not yet see everything in subjection to him [God]" (Heb. 2:8). The Christian believes that in choosing the values of Christ, the security of God is imparted to his life; but because of the victory of Christ over death, he also feels assured of the ultimate victory of God in the world. Proof and a taste of the ultimate victory have, in fact, already been given: the victory of his Saviour is the source of the Christian's freedom. A Christian's primary concern is extending God's freedom in Christ to all men so that the world men create among themselves will be more obviously God's world.

V I

In Defense of God

IF THE POSITION taken in the last two chapters be accepted, a complete denial of the "secular meaning" of the Gospel follows. The Christian Gospel has a total concern for the secular world, but the Gospel is able to be good news within that world because the Gospel brings meaning from beyond it to it. The secular world is a product of man's special activities. We can never discover our whole selves—or God—within it because we—and God—are not our own products. As makers, we are more than we make.

No creation of man is able to satisfy him. Artists, authors, musicians, poets, lovers, friends, constantly find more to say than they have said. People may save (or finance through a loan company) for years in order to pay for the car of their dreams, but by the time the car is paid for newer models are on the market, making them dissatisfied with the one they finally own. St. Augustine spoke of the restlessness of the human heart, and who can deny the accuracy of his words? Nothing ever contains us; we always want more. Professor John Wild has written: "Our human existence is marked by an openness to what is other that constantly goads it beyond itself, and that justifies the now familiar judgment that man is never what he 'is' but is always 'beyond' himself, his patterns and his ideas. This being-open-to-otherness first stretches man into a spatio-temporal world-field where he encounters things and persons radically different from himself. It enables him to love them and hate them in different ways, depending on his needs and the accidents of his history. Then it leads him to remove himself from such immediate attachments and to question their meaning. Why are things only this way and not otherwise? What is the meaning of these brute facts?"[1]

Transcendence is not the bane of religion; it is the basis of it—as it is the basis of all distinctively human meaning. We have seen that our being inexorably drives us beyond any given state of ourselves or our world. Our insatiability is an experienced fact, thus it is reasonable for us to ask the question "Why?" about it. Experiencing our transcendence within the world, we have all the material necessary—and all the motivation possible—for acknowledging the Transcendent. We are aware of our own transcendence and we also know the difference between "partial" and "total"; "total transcendence" is thus a reasonable notion for us to have. But there is more to be said in its favor than that.

The movement of our lives within the world indicates that we were made for something beyond the world. In our freedom we long for order; all of our activities—scientific, aesthetic, moral, philosophical, technological, medical, commercial, governmental, social, personal—seek to impose and discover order. But the order we achieve in the world is never sufficient for our whole person or for all persons. Worldly order is no match for our freedom; empires, theoretical systems, art forms, idioms of all sorts, techniques, ideals, are constantly challenged by the human spirit which can find no ultimate satisfaction in their limited scope. Freedom needs a context within which to express itself, but it needs a context adequate to itself. The discrepancy of order and freedom, of spirit and its context, within the world shows the insufficiency of the being of this world; it also shows the insufficiency of this-worldly living.

The whole movement of our being seeks its completion in consummate Being where freedom and order, person and context, coincide. In such a unity life is complete but not dull; no inadequacies can exist in it. God is a different kind of being than we are, but we should rejoice at that fact, for if he were not different he could not be God. That is where the unrecognized anthropo-

[1] John Wild, "An Existential Argument for the Divine Transcendence," *The Journal of Bible and Religion*, XXX, 4 (October, 1962), p. 271).

morphism of the secularist's desire for conceptual clarity leads him astray: if we won't let God be himself by being different from us we are, in effect, left only with ourselves—and that is where all of our trouble begins!

God's difference from us constitutes his transcendence. The nature of that transcendence is one of the most misunderstood tenets of "classical" Christian theology, a misunderstanding which reflects on the teaching done in seminaries as well as the teaching done—or left undone—in parishes. Transcendence does not—and never did in classical thought!—mean spatial separation or "out-thereness." Such an interpretation is a popular misunderstanding. Transcendence means, and always has meant, *difference*; God's transcendence means that his being cannot be simply identified with the being of the universe. God's transcendence opposes pantheism, not intimacy. God is always *here* (it is his transcendence—the fact that he is different enough from us to be able to *create* and *sustain* us—which enables him to be here), but he is here as different from, and thus refreshing to, us.

The existence of a transcendent God is the most reasonable explanation of the energy we find within us that drives us beyond the finite order of the world. God's existence is thus indicated by, and answers to, the concrete motion of our being. Traditional arguments for the existence of God have always been based on the direct apprehension of the nature of our being. Those arguments were frequently stated in abstract terms, but the terms were not thought to be the arguments any more than God was thought to be nothing more than the conclusion of the arguments. The arguments, as formally stated, described a lived apprehension that had to be concretely experienced. God has always been known through full-blooded experience, not just talk. To speak of present-day arguments for the existence of God as if they are the first concrete, experiential arguments shows the speaker's misreading of history rather than the superiority of present apologists. The truth of the matter is that we have generally lost the knack for examining our being in its immediacy, thus arguments whose power of persuasion is based on such an examination (as the "traditional" arguments are) lose their force for us. Our loss, however, is usually disguised as "their deficiency."

God always exists. An argument for his existence, consequently, does not draw him out of a hat; instead, such an argument tries explicitly to point out the structure involved in our prereflective awareness of him. Where is such an awareness found? In our own transcendence, is one answer. A more traditional-sounding answer is "in the awareness of contingency." Both answers are variations of the same theme.

We are able to know necessary being *immediately but indirectly* in our most basic apprehension of the being which we *are*. Necessary being is a different kind of being than we are, but the two are not unrelated; in our most immediate awareness of ourselves we realize that we cannot be ourselves by ourselves. The wholly other is somehow present with us, enabling us, and all being like us, to be ourselves. Our full experience of the inadequacy of contingent being is our indirect experience of necessary being—the only kind of experience of it we have.

In a calm mood we must deliberately fix our attention on the being we are—on the being which is us. In so doing we will become aware that we are not the totality of being and that, in fact, we need not be at all. Our being is not necessary and yet we exist; we have being, but since we are not Being, our existence is threatened and insecure. Contemplating our threatened being, we realize that if all being were like us absurdity would destroy us. *Some* being *must* be; there is no alternative to it. We know we are not such Being; and, since the insufficiency of our being is part of the universe's being, we know at the same time that the universe is not absolute Being either.[2] Within the immediate apprehension of our limited being we discover the necessity of *Being*. That discovery takes careful, sustained attention; it will be a difficult activ-

[2] At first sight our analysis may seem to commit the logical fallacy of composition which mistakenly argues from the nature of a part to the nature of a whole. If we tried to argue that because the American army had in it the biggest soldier in the world the American army was the biggest army in the world, we would commit that fallacy. The fallacy, however, is possible only where formal natures are being considered; the formal nature of a whole is often different from that of its parts. An army has different characteristics from the individuals who compose it. The fallacy does not work where *existence* is concerned. The universe has no existence as a whole apart from the existence of its parts, thus characteristics of the existence of its parts must be characteristic of *it*.

ity for those used to the excitement of rushing on in their thoughts from one thing to another, but the discovery is possible with effort—and it is necessary for wisdom!

We must quickly admit that from the indirect recogniton of necessary being we have just described we cannot tell precisely what such being is like in itself. Still, not knowing the internal nature of necessary being does not in any way attenuate the certainty of its existence. When we fully know contingent being, we know through *its* nature *that* necessary being must be: an experience of the "whatness" of the one involves the recognition of the "thatness" of the other. "Clearness to us" is not the criterion for the existence of anything except in certain language-games we choose to play; but when the playing is over and we consider the being that engulfs us with our games, that being's Source must be both real and mysterious.

The peculiarity of the first person singular pronoun and the *finality* of such statements as "I'm I" and "I do it because I'm I," which were admitted to be necessary for the secular meaning of the Gospel, we found to be manifestations of a transcending mystery recognized even in our daily lives. Persons are sources of activity that transcend their expression and all the external circumstances in which they find themselves; that is where the *finality* of "I'm I" comes from. Even in this world personal transcendence is mysterious, for we can never *capture* it in our tests or concepts. But even though—or, more truly, *because*—we cannot capture it, it is the origin of everything truly satisfying to us.

When a man gives a woman an engagement ring and she accepts it, the significance of their action is not exhausted by the ring— no matter how much was paid for it. The true value of their relationship transcends the limited, external act and is rooted in the inexhaustibility of their free, personal selves.

In love, two subjects will their union with each other in the depths of their being. Love is not content with "I"; it requires "we." In willing to be united with you in love, I am in a most important sense *willing you*. Love is thus seen to be the ultimate ground of creation because, in being itself, it naturally tends to posit the other as other. Human love cannot completely posit another person in his being, but it shows its intention of doing so by the delight it takes in the beloved's presence. God's love, because it is omnipotent, can posit the being of the beloved in its totality; what is only a tendency in our love is an actuality in his. Love does not suppress the singularity of the other; as we have indicated, it requires the singularity of the other in order to be itself. Sartre perverts love's nature when he describes it in terms of "capturing" or making the beloved less than himself.

Two people in love actually will the being of each other and show that will by delighting in each other. The intrigue, challenge, and freshness of love result from the fact that the two subjects uniting in it are centers of freedom whose creativity and newness can never be exhausted. Love is the true mystery of life because it involves persons in the deepest mystery of their being.

The statement "I'm I" is not a vacuous tautology; instead, it is the mark of an *inexhaustible subject*. The inexhaustibility of a personal subject is quite different from the inexhaustibility proper to physical reality, however: persons are inexhaustible where they are; matter is inexhaustible only in its extension beyond a given place. To locate a person is to locate a mystery, to encounter transcendence. God's transcendence is his inexhaustibility. Such a statement is not nonsense to us because every truly personal relationship we have in the world supplies us with justification for it.

It should be clear by now that in any analysis of religion the transcendent movement of man's spirit must be distinguished from its limited external expression. After recognizing that religion is a living phenomenon in the world, the secularist tries to capture its whole significance in its material expression. The life of religion, however, is found in the total movement of the spirit through its expressions, not in the formal expression alone; once that movement is abstracted only a lifeless corpse remains. The secularist does not actually study the thing he starts out to investigate; he destroys it instead. Unaware that he has killed his subject, he moves from the inadequacy of the dead expression with which he is left to the impossibility of the activity which first caught his attention. A non sequitur if there ever was one.

Subjectivity cannot exist without expression and can be known only through its expression, but it is always more than its expression. Religion involves us as subjects with God as Subject; thus religious activity is more than, and escapes, complete expression. Secular analysis is predicated on the assumption that the *lived* can be reduced to the *representative*: what cannot be represented in scientific terms is said not to exist in empirical reality. Such an explicative method is incapable of studying religion because it cannot recognize religion for what it is in itself.

Once the totality of our relationship with God is established and God is recognized as the Source of all beings, the problem of how he speaks to us is considerably eased. God does not need to speak to us in a special way, in a special kind of knowing as the secularist contends; God speaks to us in all ways, in all kinds of knowing. The experience of Christians through the ages is that God can inspire them, and thus speak to them, through everything he allows to happen to them. The problem of religious inspiration is not how it is given, but how it is received; it is given everywhere to those who can appreciate being's transcendental dimension. Pierre Teilhard de Chardin's awareness of God in his scientific work is a notorious example of such appreciation.

God would be "destroyed by a thousand qualifications" only if he were a finite object in the world. As transcendent Source of the world, there are always a thousand affirmations we can make about him for every thousand qualifications of our mode of referring to him. He transcends us in his Perfection; he differs from us by excess of perfection rather than by defect or negation, as we differ from one another—and from God. You and I differ from each other because of the imperfections of our being; each of us is something the other is not. You may be an astronomer, I an historian; you a musician, I a writer; you a tennis player, I a gardener; you active, I inactive; you fair complexioned, I medium complexioned; you young, I middle-aged. Because my being does not contain your perfection, you differ from me. God differs from us through the fullness of his being rather than through the incompleteness of it; negation can neither touch nor destroy him. Negation refers only to us, to our mode of being and our way of knowing him.

We have seen that a significant statement is one that says something. In order to affirm *something*, however, something else must be denied. On that criterion statements about God are meaningful because they exclude all imperfection from him. The world of our everyday experience is a mixed world; the perfections found in it are mixed with negations. It is precisely the mixed nature of ourselves and the world that leads us to see the necessity of an unmixed Source to account for us and it. But how does "accounting" or "explaining" work? When one thing explains another, we find that the thing doing the explaining never has the characteristics that are to be explained. The molecular theory, for example, explains the process of burning because molecules themselves do not burn; atoms explain molecules, in turn, because atoms do not have the characteristics molecules have; subatomic particles explain atoms, but they are able to do so only to the extent they do not have the characteristics atoms have. Now physicists are looking for something still *different* to explain the few properties which remain of subatomic particles. When we understand that even in the physical sciences explanation proceeds through difference, the explanatory role of "difference" in theology is seen not to be the absurd thing critics say it is. To be sure, God's difference is a unique type of difference, but that is a point in his favor—not against him.

Because all the perfections of which we are directly aware are mixed perfections, concepts based on them cannot be referred directly to God. Thus the problem of religious language arises: we cannot see God as the clear object of our knowledge. The secularist is so disappointed by this situation that he tries to use it as a disproof of God's existence and a proof of the meaninglessness of the word "God." The committed Christian, on the other hand, takes the inability we have just mentioned as the confirmation of his religious insight rather than as its disproof. Religious people are not totally immobilized by the impotency of their concepts and the fact that they cannot know God as an object, for their spiritual activity aims at a God beyond concepts and objects in the first place. Knowing the life of the spirit to be more than its expression, they do not confuse inadequacies of expression for total inabilities of the spirit.

Our participation in being is richer than our powers of abstract reflection. Once we exist we can reflect upon our existence, but our "insertion into being" lies beyond our clear, conceptual grasp. Reason works pretty well with what is present to it, but the beginning and end of things drives it to myth—if not to distraction. We could clearly understand our insertion into being if we understood Being-itself, our Source, but we cannot. Since God transcends all of his worldly expression, since, in other words, we cannot know him as we know objects in the world, St. Thomas Aquinas said that he must be known *by participation* rather than by abstraction.[3] St. Thomas means that God cannot be known through our ideas alone but only through our being; the way we participate in existence leads us to the living God.

Our participation in being is from a Source other than ourselves —that is what we mean when we say God is our Cause. God's causality does not work the same way causes do within our universe, but since a cause, as the term can be most generally understood, is anything that makes a positive contribution to the being of another, we cannot deny its fitting—although not restricting —application to God. The subject of analogy must come up again, for we can say that God is the Cause of the universe only in an analogical manner. No other cause can be exactly like him, but other causes can be themselves only be*cause* of him. "Dependency" is a relation arising out of causation; it is the relation of an effect to its cause. The dependency of our universe and ourselves upon our transcendent Source means that God is somehow our Cause.

We know that we are not Being; to have being, but not to be being, indicates that we *participate* in it. We are only participations of the perfections we have, for we do not possess them completely in their own names. I have reason, but I am not reason; I have being, but I am not being. Since our being is willed to us by another (for we must remember that the Christian God is Love, not an impersonal thing), the nature of our being cannot totally mislead us about the nature of our Source. God does not

[3] St. Thomas Aquinas, *In Librum Beati Dionysii De Divinis Nominibus*, C. Pera, ed. (Turin-Rome: Marietti, 1950), Cap. II, lect. 4, #176.

resemble us in the limited modes in which we have our perfections, but we do resemble him in whatever perfection we have: we must resemble him in the existential sense to which we are referring, for we come completely from him. Our resemblance is our dependence! Every effect so resembles its cause. A table does not look like a carpenter, but because carpenters can make tables, tables tell us something about carpenters. We do not look like God, but, because God is our Source, our being tells us something about ("resembles" in the sense we are using the term) him. Our being, properly understood, points us toward God, but to point toward him as our transcendent Source is not to capture him as our bagged prize.

"Pointing" is an appropriate way of apprehending transcendence, for both pointing and transcendence are directional. In the direction we transcend the material world as persons, God transcends us; that is why knowing God through personal analogy is the best kind of knowledge we can have of him. Yet as Source of ALL, God not only transcends us in the *direction* our personal being transcends the material world, he even transcends the direction! Although there is a special appropriateness in our referring to God in personal terms, we must not make him less than himself in such reference. God can become so rarefied in our thought that he does not have the attractiveness full-bodied persons do. We must remember that, although God as our Source is different from us, he *is* not *thin*—he is not less than the universe, but more. Our lives as persons are interesting because of the variety we find in the world; life in God does not lose that richness. Our approach to God through *all of the perfection and variety of the universe* is necessary because he is in himself all the perfection of the universe and more. God's being encompasses the perfection of fire's warmth and the beauty of a sunset without being either a fire or a star, just as he is the perfection of person without being a human being.

When we speak of God's "warmth" and "depth," his "freshness" and "vitality," even his "colorfulness" and "sweetness," we are speaking metaphorically. But such metaphors give *thickness* to God by helping us relate ourselves to him in the totality of our being. God is more than we are, not less—he differs from us, we said, by excess not by negation and defect—but as theology usually talks about him he becomes so abstract that he seems less, not more, than personal. We cannot help losing interest in such a god. When religion is understood to originate from the total movement of our being toward our transcendent Source, when verbal expression is understood not to contain religion (because it is only a vehicle used by the spirit to ground and locate its transcending life), we discover an exhilarating freedom in the terminology we can use.

Not confusing itself with its expression, the living spirit may express itself with an abandon that scandalizes a conventionally bound secular observer. Freedom is not an excuse for inconsistency, but once the primacy of the spirit over its expression is recognized, *the consistency of that transcendence through all formal expression* allows the spirit to combine formal expressions at a level of consistency exceeding their limited capacities. Religious intentionality is defined more by the object toward which it tends than by the formal consistency of its isolated expressions. Thus metaphors can meaningfully be applied to God while they are recognized to be metaphors. There *is* truth in the Christian's staggering realization that "God gave himself for me."

Nicholas of Cusa's reference to God as the "coincidence of opposites" must be understood along these lines. Nicholas did not mean that God is a hodge-podge of contradictions; he meant, rather, that since God completely transcends the world he transcends the relative opposition of all perfections in the world. God "moves" and is "stationary," "hears" and is "heard," "sees" and is "seen," is "big" and is "small," "touches" and is "touched," is "hidden" and is "known" because he transcends the level of reality at which limited perfections are opposed to each other. To say that God is the coincidence of opposites is to say that God transcends the level of all opposition. Such transcendence is mysterious to our relative mode of being, but it is that toward which we are oriented in our being.

Contrary to popular expectation, many of the problems we have in religion come not from God's transcendence but from the fact that we will not let him be transcendent enough. The movement of our being and our deepest grasp of the nature of contingency show *that* God exists. Knowing that he is, our natural inclination is to want to know as clearly as possible what he is. When we try to clarify his nature in a specific way, however, we tend to make him so much like ourselves that his existence as God becomes an impossibility. We make our own problems by surreptitiously circumscribing him in our attempts to understand him. Because the problems *we* have appear to be problems about *his* existence (as we project our difficulties into his nature), the problems some people have in conceptualizing God lead them to deny his existence.

God exists for us as mystery. The consequences of that fact are further reaching than many people realize. We cannot first affirm God's existence, secondly affirm his mystery, and then go on to understand other things about him clearly! The lesson of God's transcendence is that everything about him is mysterious; if his thorough difference from us is understood, we will not be misled to think that we can understand some aspects of his nature better than others.

The truly religious dimension, in my opinion, is conspicuous by its absence in certain recent criticisms of the doctrine of the Trinity. Just as it is easier to tell jokes about people than to understand them, so it is easier to tell jokes about the Trinity than to understand the doctrine. The disheartening thing is that jokes about misinterpretations of the Trinity have been used to discredit a doctrine that, if understood, would make the jokes impossible. The Trinity can be jokingly ridiculed for implying a "committee God" only if there is some basis for employing the words "person" and "committee" about God in the same way that they are applied to human persons and committees. To get the confusions of a human committee out of the triune nature of the Christian God is to base one's humor on such a sad misinterpretation of Christian intentionality that the comedy becomes a tragedy. St. Augustine has sometimes been accused of trying to make the Trinity too clear, of trying to explain it too thoroughly, but he—if not his critics—knew the minimal nature of what he was saying. He accepted orthodox usage and spoke of three "Persons" in the Trinity, without feeling he was a polytheist, because he knew he was not speaking univocally about God at all. He wrote: "We use the expression three Persons, or three substances, not to suggest any difference in essence, but to furnish ourselves with some one word by which to answer the question: *What* are these 'three'?"[4] In other words, St. Augustine used "Persons" in his explication of the Trinity because there was no other word to use, not because "Persons" adequately explained God. Impersonal words do not tell enough about God's power to be our best guides to his interior nature, but even personal words, in fact, even the word "person," can only serve as analogical indications of his eminence.

The vehemence of some criticism of Christian doctrine seems possible only to the extent that the critic is more guilty of the mistake he is criticizing, viz., the overspecification of God by man, than the condemned position. *Everything* about God is mysterious. Some who reject the doctrine of the Trinity are willing, nevertheless, to accept the Fatherhood of God, but if it is really the Fatherhood *of God* they accept, that Fatherhood is no less mysterious and transcendent than the Trinity is! The Fatherhood of God as revealed to us by Christ can reasonably be accepted when the religious intention of "Fatherhood" is grasped, but it is no more difficult, I suggest, to accept the Christian doctrine of the Trinity when its religious intention is understood.

When we speak of God as "Father," we use a human word to direct our attention toward God as the transcendent Source and Creator of all things; God is not a father the way human beings are. Still the word has a foundation in reality for indicating an aspect of God's mystery. Referring to God as "Trinity" has a similar foundation and a similar function. Christians know God as Love, Life, Fecundity. God's Fatherhood, in fact, is characterized by those very terms. To claim that God is Love is perhaps the most common insight of Christians, but love, we have seen, is a perfection requiring relationship between persons. The perfection

[4] From *Augustine: Later Works, LCC*, Vol. VIII, ed. by John Burnaby (London: SCM Press Ltd., 1955; Philadelphia: The Westminster Press, 1955), p. 38. Used by permission.

itself is social and requires a distinction of persons; if God is to *be* Love, his transcendent perfection must somehow embrace within it a distinction of persons without their separation (for separation is an imperfection). Such a relationship is exactly what love allows, however, for it is a *union* which overcomes separation while at the same time intensifying distinction. People become *one* in love, but their very union requires their continued distinctness. Dialogue, love, knowledge, fecundity, community, companionship, concern, openness, availability, communication, presence, are all perfections of being which must somehow be found in God. The doctrine of the Trinity is Christianity's most inclusive and self-sufficient means of expressing the personal and social "inclusiveness" of the transcendent Source of reality. In the Trinity, Persons indwell Persons; "person," the ultimate explanatory principle, thus becomes the context for itself. In that way the perfection and absolute sufficiency of God's Being are expressed for man in ultimate terms. The Trinity is the best means we have of showing how freedom and order, person and context, coincide in God.

The doctrine of the Trinity is more basic than the doctrine of God's fatherhood of the world, for the Trinity indicates how God can be our Father. God is able to create things "outside" himself and be their Father because he lives a life of eternal "begetting" and "bestowing" within himself. His activity in creating and giving himself to a world that differs from him mirrors the fecundity of his Being within himself; his Being is Word, Love, Dialogue, Life, thus the doctrine of the Trinity helps us appreciate the source and force of his love for us. Even the transcendent God is not too great to be bothered with us, for his Being is Personal Concern.

The fullness and sufficiency of God's personal life within himself, as shown by the doctrine of the Trinity, indicate his absolute freedom in the creation of the world. He did not have to create the universe in order to escape "loneliness" and "solitude." The total absence of necessity on God's part in creating indicates that the only reason for his act of creation is his love. Love is free; perfect Love is perfectly free. The understanding that God's only motivation in creating is to manifest his love, calls us to the fullest lives of love and thanksgiving of which we are capable. The nature of God has the most immediate influence on the nature of our lives in the world. Certainly the doctrine of the Trinity does not "at best" lead to a "sense of irrelevance," as has recently been charged. The Trinity keeps God from being irrelevant because it shows that ultimate Reality itself is Love and Self-giving—exactly the life to which Christ calls us! That is why Christian theology maintains that the Incarnation can be understood only within the doctrine of the Trinity.

There is a lot to be said for Austin Farrer's suggestion that the doctrine of the Trinity should be received by us as an *image* rather than as a conceptual explication of God. The scriptural image of a Son (or Lamb) standing before the eternal throne of the Father receiving the sevenfold gift of the Spirit must be accepted or rejected as significant in its entirety.[5] An image has a self-contained meaning; it will do us no good conceptually to try to get within it in order to understand how the Son got before the throne and precisely how the Spirit is given to him. In the image to which we are referring the Son is simply before the Father receiving the Spirit. The doctrine of the Trinity, because it is about God, is so mysterious that we cannot crawl within it and learn point by point how the Son and Holy Spirit are Persons proceeding from the Father. There is a special appropriateness to God's revealing himself to us in images, for they have a concreteness about them which speaks directly to us as persons. An image or symbol can be lived because it collects the whole man and speaks to him in his wholeness: a man will die for a symbol of the reality in which he believes much more readily than he will die for a theory about that reality. Symbols and images call for a type of participation completely bypassed by abstract theories; symbols focus our lives in a way thought alone cannot. They are, accordingly, the most fitting way for a God "above" us to impress us and communicate his mystery to us. We get rest and challenge, satisfaction and intrigue, from images; they encourage and dare us at the same time, for they are both informative and provocative at once.

[5] Cf. Austin Farrer, *The Glass of Vision* (Westminster: Dacre Press, 1958), Lecture III.

The completeness of God's difference from us, when understood in the Christian sense, has the most amazing consequences for our lives in the world—amazing, that is, to secularists and to some who call themselves Christians with too much ease. God's transcendence, instead of removing him from us and making him unimportant to us, is what enables him to be most intimately present with us; only the *difference* of his being enables him to be immanent everywhere in the world. God's revealed message to us in the Incarnation is that our only chance for relation with him is through the world. *His difference drives us into the world: his being is so unlike ours that we have no means of conceiving an approach to him outside the world.* We *must* love him through the world for lack of an alternative!

By means of the Incarnation of his Son, God the Father tells us in his own Word that we can get to him only through creation. God tells us that we will be most like him if we will be most fully ourselves in the world through his Spirit. The Incarnation animates the world with God, imparting God's security to our lives; and it enables us to relate ourselves to the transcendent God through the specificity of the world. ". . . he who does not love his brother whom he has seen, how can he love God whom he has not seen?" (I John 4:20).

VII

Religious Living

It HAS been said that people today face identity crises. We have tried to point out that such crises are frequently precipitated because we try to live in incomplete, partial "worlds of man" instead of in our whole, proper world. Only frustration can result from trying to live complete lives in worlds that are defined primarily by the way they abstract from human fullness.

Our world is one in which we can participate with all our being; that is the kind of world religion requires too. Such a world is first of all one we can see, hear, touch, taste, and smell. It is a world of sex, food, beauty, virtue, vice, love, hate, hope, fear, pleasure, pain, expectation, disappointment, pride, humility, boredom. It is one in which we become tired and seek rest; it is one in which we feel energetic and become ambitious. It is a world of passionate and emotional motivation as well as of intellectual insight and understanding. It is a world in which a man probes the expanse of the universe and the depth of the atom in order to move into a new house and buy a better car. It is a world in which hypocrisy is more powerful than mathematics, where selfishness is called liberty.

We can be ourselves only in *our* world, but we are located in that world through our bodies and must be in one special place at one special time. That is why we are forced to make decisions in our lives; we cannot have—or be—everything at once.

Decision and the identity it brings, not size and the deception it brings, are the necessary ingredients of personal living. Christian love may be as genuinely shown in a small kindness as in a great sacrifice. The important thing is that specific deeds, such as being patient with a child or pledging friendship to a persecuted person, testify through their *actuality* to the actuality of God's love for us in Christ. There is no Christian alternative to specific actions. The importance of doing what one can, but doing something, is impressively taught in the feeding of the five thousand: with so many people present and only a few fishes and barley loaves at hand, Andrew asked Jesus, ". . . what are they among so many?" (John 6:9). Doing what they could and using what they had, however, a problem bigger than their resources could handle was solved God's way. The Father's call to us in Christ is to live *decisively* for him as Christ lived and as he taught his disciples to live. Such living will involve all the decisions we make in the world, but that is why God puts us in a world—so we can specifically love him through the world's concreteness.

The Christian God is a creating and redeeming God, who shows himself from first to last by his acts of love in the world. Christianity stresses that God in turn must be loved in and through the world, not apart from it. The Son of God consummated his revelation of the Father by giving his life for the world. That being the case, it seems improbable that Christians should have problems relating their religion to the world or thinking they could be religious apart from their full lives in it. But as improbable as it seems, the ingenuity of man has triumphed! That is exactly what has happened.

An incarnational religion cannot be a "ghostly religion."

True enough. But that only shows that a ghostly religion cannot be Christianity. How can we account for the ethereal character of many people's religion?

I think we have suggested a way in this book. The meaning of Christianity is lost for many people because they have lost the full understanding of what it is to be a human person. Because they do not understand the radical nature of man's location in the world they do not understand the relation of religious—or any—meaning to the world. Just as man as a person is not complete in himself and then put into a world that is completely itself without him, so thought is not complete in itself and then put into words or some other form of external expression that is totally separate from it. As we are ourselves through our bodies, so our thoughts are their full selves only through their expression.

Maurice Merleau-Ponty can once more supply us with suggestive insights. He maintains that our thought is somehow *in* the words we use and *in* the actions we perform. Meaning is not found completely self-contained behind our external words and actions. Is it not true that we most fully understand our thoughts when they are put into words? Do we not find that ideas which at first excited us with their possibilities sometimes turn out to be disappointing when we have written them down? I've had the experience many times in writing this book! In such cases it is through our *words* that we discover the deficiency of our *thoughts*. Does that not show that our thought is somehow *in* our words? It is also through words that we learn new ideas from other people. If a person's thought was not embodied in his words, how could we learn his thoughts *from* his words?

There are aspects of thought that transcend words, but that is not to deny that our thought reaches a type of completion in words. If we understood that all meaning is most fully itself in its expression, we would understand religious meaning's need for external expression as one instance of a general rule.

But we have not yet said all that is needed. Words are a form of external expression, and that is exactly the difficulty. Many people think that talking and reading about religion are all they have to do to be religious. It is the element of *totality* in religion that they miss.

Because, in Christianity, we see ourselves and our world as a totality related to the transcendent God, nothing can be removed from our religious concern. The Christian Word is a Person. As that Word calls us, we can answer him only with the words that are our persons—and we as persons are relation-to-the-world. Christian meaning cannot be found in abstract thoughts alone.

Because life in Christ is meaning given to us from our transcendent Source, that meaning remakes us and our world rather than merely informing our intellects. It is meaning so immediately related to us that our only hope is to *be* it. Since it issues from the Source of all reality it is meaning we can never lose (for nothing can fall outside of it), and it is meaning we can never discover (for it can be received only as a gift through revelation). In receiving it we immediately participate in it and belong to it: it is our most personal means of participating in the God who creates and sustains us. The meaning-of-God-in-Christ speaks to the whole person and can itself be spoken only by the whole person. That the Christ-life is the ultimate value in which we can participate is the lesson of Christ's resurrection from the dead. Jesus' physical resurrection showed that, through him, God the Father wills to perfect and sustain, in time everlasting, our whole lives of personal-participation-in-the-world as we actually live them through our bodies. We will never be worldless. The meaning of Easter and the empty tomb is that our new world after death will be found through Jesus Christ and *his* relation to the Father.

Many Christians, by "overspiritualizing" their answers to the problems of the Church and of the world, keep their solutions from applying to the very problems they set out to solve. If we *falsely* spiritualize our Christianity by ignoring the relation of the spiritual aspects of our being to our physical aspects (in all strictness, we cannot overspiritualize Christianity—just underemphasize other aspects of it), we will end by ignoring the totality of our human condition as it actually exists. That means that people who recognize their difficulties and problems to be manifestations of the human condition will not recognize the religion we advocate as any viable solution for them. With a warped or over- or underdeveloped understanding of the human condition, we also lose the full significance of God's saving action taken for us by Jesus Christ, the Incarnate Lord.

Christian theologians are fond of stating that a unique insight of the Jews was the realization that God reveals himself in history.[1] In his dealings with his chosen people, the Supreme and Mighty God, Absolute Ruler of the Universe, always said specific things in specific circumstances through specific men. Through the patri-

[1] Cf. Henry Duméry, *Phénoménologie et religion* (Paris: Presses Universitaires de France, 1958), pp. 12 ff.

archs, judges, Samuel, Saul, David, Solomon, Amos, Hosea, Micah, and the whole prophetic development, the Israelites learned that they were living with God through their daily lives in the world.

The Judaic-Christian tradition has always had its great heroes and saints, but here again God's historical way of dealing with men is evident. Old and New Testament heroes are "types" who we think should be emulated, but they were not fictitious types before they were men. They were men who became types. Think, for example, of Abraham, Moses, David, Jeremiah, Thomas, Matthew, Andrew. Christian saints are not mythical heroes whose broad outlines were filled in to make them seem human. (The trouble with many of them was that they were so human—even our Lord—that some people—think of the apocryphal gospels—wanted to make them less human than they were.) Saints are *first* human beings in whom the action of God becomes so obvious that, through their particularities and imperfections, we are able to see the *type* of God's working with man. Think of St. Peter, St. Francis of Assisi, St. Teresa of Avila; they were real people whose reality is a primary source of their attractiveness.

Because God's action in Christ is meant to extend to all men—and has notoriously been so extended in the lives of those whom we recognize to be saints—Christian Truth must be communicable and continuous throughout history. The Church as a community and institution has its origin in that fact.

Being the Mystical Body of Christ, the Church plays a role in the world of today analogous to the role played by Christ's natural body when he lived in Galilee. *The Church locates God's action in the world.* Persons always live in specific places; they never just are. They are always *there*—or *here*. The givenness of our location is known as our facticity.

The role the body plays in our individual lives, in turn, is played by laws and institutions in our social lives. It is foolish, an attempt to be less than human, to think that we can be persons apart from institutions and traditions, whether inside or outside of our religious activities. Laws and institutions are residues of personal living that locate us in one specific communal and cultural place rather than another. Laws and institutions—as a physical body—

are necessary if we are to be ourselves: we have to be someplace culturally and religiously as well as physically.

Such was Israel's insight into the institutional and communal nature of religion. *The continuity and objectivity of religious institutions do not keep us from God; they locate us in our approach to God.* The Jew knew that he had a personal relation to God only because of his incorporation into a community that bore continuing marks of God's choice of it. Institutions and laws show that God has something to say to his people. But we must go further.

To be a person is not just to be *in* or *at*; it is to be *beyond* and *through*. Personal being, as we have stressed so often, is itself only insofar as it transcends its already-given physical and social environment. As men, we have bodies only to transcend them in personal relations. Our need to "pass beyond" does not end there, however. Our neighbors, our world, even the universe as a whole, do not fully answer our personal needs. Thus it is that we are religious creatures, relentlessly driven by our own nature (whether we consciously recognize it or not) toward God.

The mistake of certain Jews—the self-satisfied Pharisees—was to recognize the need for institutional location in religion without the correlative truth of personal transcendence. They thought their predecessors' past and God's previous acts would be their automatic passport to the future. They forgot that spiritual living knows only a transcending *present*. The time of decision for a person is always *now*, not *then*. Eastern Orthodox Christianity is especially commendable for its recognition that the Church as "community" transcends the Church as "organization," while maintaining at the same time that neither aspect exists apart from the other.

We must take our personal power of transcendence, as our bodies, seriously. We must not admit our transcendence as an opening remark and then forget it. We must relate it immediately and constantly to all we say and do; it must influence our understanding of the Church, sacraments, preaching, ministry, our whole lives. All the things we have just mentioned are only means of getting to God.

"To transcend" means "to go beyond." But "going beyond"

requires something which is passed, and a location to give the action expression and direction. "To go beyond" is never "to leave out." That is why the Christian goal of union with God properly requires the created universe and the visible Church and sacraments as its means. We transcend things *through* them, not apart from them. Personal transcendence is positive and inclusive, not negative and forgetful. That is the difference between transcendence and abstraction.

The conclusion of all we have said is that *religion is worldly*. The realization of that fact should solve people's problems about how to live their religion, but the statement is so short that it does not give people the details they need actually to practice it. Accordingly, we shall now collect various insights from our study and try to use them as a boy uses a magnifying glass to concentrate the sun's rays on paper he wants to set afire. Can the position we have suggested help concentrate rays from the "light of the world" in such a way that we will be set on fire by his love and consequently inaugurate a new epoch of Christian commitment?

A sense of purpose in religion is lacking for our age. It can be strikingly regained if we realize that we and our world are incomplete. Life in our world is not God's game of chess, played with already-made men on a completely-made board. God did not create things once upon a time, a long time ago, in order to use time up pushing them around according to rules only he knows. God's act of creation is going on now; we are in on the beginning of things because nothing is as yet final.

If we see the essential incompleteness of the world, we will have less trouble living the Christian life, for we will then see our constant *need for it*. We will see that love, joy, hope, trust, and humility must rule our lives and govern our actions because it is through our lives and actions that God is creating *his* world. We remember what we have to use—what we know we are dependent on. Religion today is easy to forget because much of the time people see no need to use it and consequently feel no dependence upon it. Have you ever studied a foreign language by yourself, knowing all the time that you would probably never use it? How easy it was to forget the vocabulary lists you memorized! If you suddenly found yourself in a country which spoke only that language, however, the story would be quite different. Similarly, to see the constant need for our religion is the way to assure its constant use.

It is because we mistakenly see the world, ourselves, and Christianity as complete, done, over with, that our religion "doesn't stay with us." Christ, for many, seems to have come, done his work, triumphed over death, and left. Such people feel God has determined a final end for them in his providence; he has given them hope about what that end will be through the resurrection of his Son; their task now is not to forget what he has shown them in the past and patiently to wait until he finishes the mysterious game he is playing in the universe. People of this type think they become Christians by trying to live in the past in the present. As a result they lose their initiative and involvement in the world. They think of themselves either as chessmen passively shoved around by the great Player in the sky, or they think of themselves as some kind of safe-deposit box in which God's past acts are to be preserved untouched for the consolation of future generations.

The truth is that we are not here to keep or to be kept, for neither we nor our world are complete enough to be preserved for what they are. Man's "natural memory" may be able to "keep things just as they were," but Christian memory is project for the future. It is not an abstract musing on the past. The attempt to relive the past in the present violates the ongoing structure of our being; we are ourselves when we live in the present for the future. Then we move with time, not against it. The truth of the past must not be overlooked in the present, but that truth exists for the future, not to keep us from the future. God made us the temporal beings we are; he set the direction of time. Living in him, time (and our being) does not contradict itself. The past will never obstruct or try to replace the future.

In the Christian life the future defines the past, not vice versa. God's incarnate acts in the past are our *tasks* for the future; they are historic marks of his timeless will *which call us into the future, if we understand the nature of their presence in the past.*

Owing to our nature as persons, just by *being* we are *creating;*

to create is why we exist, and it should be the source of our value in our eyes as it is in God's eyes. To be sure, our value as persons first comes from the fact that God creates and sustains us, but he creates us to be creators and that purpose cannot be separated from our being. *Wherever we are, the way we live is the way we are creating the world, and to be creating the world is always to be doing something important.*

We have seen that man's world is a world of values; that fact makes it a world of participation and involvement, a world utilizing every aspect of man's being, for value requires firsthand engagement to be itself. *God's will is to valorize the universe through us.* To the degree that we participate in reality around us, projecting our aims and questions into it, and receiving answers from it, that reality becomes a *world.* The universe which exists outside and beyond us is known only from within our world view and may, so to speak, be considered the raw material out of which God lets us join him as creators. The universe—our environment— is sustained by God to be used by us (and perhaps by other personal beings); it is not its full self until it has been so used. We, as part of creation, are the means by which the universe becomes its full self in the glorification of God. The turning of our environment into a world by our use and valuation of it is not something superfluous added to the universe; our lives are not furniture polish rubbed on an already-complete product, merely highlighting what is already there. The universe is incomplete until it is creatively related to God through our world.

It is in Christ that we are to become ourselves and to make the world. Action is our destiny, but it must be Christian action— action whose sole motivation is God, not ourselves. Such action is sometimes called Christian passivity, but we must not let the word "passivity" deceive us. Existence is always an act; we exist as persons in the material universe only to the extent that we make that universe our world by actualizing *human* values in it.

Our being is the doing of something (the making of world) with God; doing something with him, we can recognize our presence with him through the doing. The doing of which we speak involves all our being, thus we are present with him in all our being. We valorize the universe through our eating and drinking, courting and mating, giving and spending, governing and administrating, buying and selling, giving and taking, walking and talking, resting and sleeping, making and distributing, waiting and suffering, just as through our planning and praying. Nothing we do or undergo is useless or unimportant, for it is God's way of completing the reality of his universe through us.

Doing things together is the way we get to know one another as human beings; it is the way we discover our common nature; it gives us something to share, a purpose for being together, and something upon which to stand in the mutual love that transcends all outward expression. Creating the world with God is the way God wants us to get to know him; that activity is the privilege of our being. It is what we have in "common" with him in the sense that we are "made in his image"; it is what he offers to share with us; it is the purpose of our being, and it supplies the ground upon which we can stand in our all-transcending love of him.

To say that we must make our world, as has already been indicated, is not to deny the reality of the universe; it is rather a way of affirming the necessary task of personal presence in a physical location. We can try to live in things or we can try to live through them. To live through them is most obviously to be beyond them—which is exactly the status of a person. *Things* can always be made to say more than they have said so far, and there is always more reality through which we can speak of God's love than lies within the horizon of our present world. We must use things for God's purposes, transforming and making personal instruments of them, and we must constantly strive to enlarge our world in our never-ceasing dialogue with the being beyond us. As human beings, we never "have it made": neither we nor our world is finished.

St. Paul said in his Second Epistle to the Corinthians: ". . . through Christ our consolation overflows" (1:5, NEB.). Participation in Christ is the value which consummates our lives. *Living in him, he overflows us, and so creates the world through us.* Such making is, in effect, a remaking when its results are compared to the world men make without Christ. Christian living is thus the *redemption* of the world—its true humanization—because our God-intended nature is found only in Christ. The way the world is humanized is by divine help; the world becomes "fit" for man —becomes his suitable home—only by means of something more than him. But, by making the world man's in this manner, it becomes more obviously God's, for God is the source and strength of the values that constitute man. We live God's love by completing the world with the Son's perfections. Sharing and choosing our values in the Son, we are most truly one with each other and with the Father. Living in this way, we participate in the stability of God, whose beauty is holiness, and we participate in the work of the Son, who redeems the world by giving us his Spirit.

Life with God is involvement with the world for God—not shutting out the world in order to be with God. God is so much more than we are, and our dependence upon him is so total, that we cannot adequately know him or our relation to him through abstract ideas. Our whole being is a type of participation in him, thus we can most adequately know him through the participation which is our whole being. There is no possibility of reducing participation to anything less than involvement!

Involvement with our whole being in the world is our Christian destiny; anything less than that will keep us from relating to God in a Christlike manner. Such involvement in the world will tax us, wear us out, but only when we are so taxed and worn out will our needs be obvious enough to us for us to see that God is the only answer for us. A question must be real before its answer can be real. We do not really ask about God in our usual "search" for him, for we do not want him to be our *all*. Our usual desire is to remain what we are and have him "finish off" the few places we are not satisfied with ourselves. Most of us have what can be called a "plaster religion." We want God to repair the cracks in our lives when they appear, but when our foundations have not been shaken we want him to remain in the cupboard out of the way.

We want God to sugar-coat our core, but, unknown to us, the core of our being needs changing rather than coating. If we live

with God in the core of our being, the latter's forward thrust will
show itself as *trust* in God, and its affirmation will be one with
humility. When time becomes trust, the sacraments will *become*
our lives; there will be no discrepancy between time and trust—
the sacraments and life—in which doubt, despair, or anxiety can
dwell.

Properly understood, the sacraments are not empty shells or
formal ceremonies separated from our lives that we must fill with
meaning from our lives. Sacraments are the meaning-content of
the Christian life at the level at which that life must be lived; they
are the filling of life with the meaning of Christ. The sacraments,
in addition to their bestowal of grace, are *commissions* given to us
from God, through Christ's mystical Body the Church, to continue
everywhere the work of Christ's glorified body which is now in
heaven.[2] The identity of the two bodies—the mystical and the
glorified—means that through our incorporation into the Church
we *are* Christ's action in the world. We are centers of his presence.
Such Christian work cannot be done by reflection alone; it is the
work of our whole selves living in the power of the Holy Spirit.

In a most significant sense the eucharistic action is not an action once performed and then discontinued until the Eucharist is
done again at the altar. Each Eucharist is a charge laid upon the
People of God through the Body (as Church) by the Body (as
Food) to live the eucharistic action everywhere in the world.
Grace is continually offered to us by God to live the eucharistic
action throughout our lives. We may leave the place of our com-
missioning (the altar), but we cannot leave the commission itself
—or God's ever-present offer of grace to accomplish it. The sacraments indicate the nature of God's constant will for man. God
does not become inactive when a sacrament is "completed" at a
church service. The *outward signs* of his purpose for us may come
and go as we participate in church services, but the concern and
offer of help continue on God's part—as the action is meant to
continue on our part.

Until we learn that meaning is *in* its external expression, until

[2] Cf. E. Schillebeeckx, *Christ the Sacrament of the Encounter with God*
(New York: Sheed & Ward, 1963), *passim.*

we learn that meaning is not itself apart from its embodiment, as we are not ourselves apart from our embodiment, we will never know how to live the Christian life. *Creating the world and living the sacraments are the same act.* Both are complete and incomplete at the same time: complete in respect to God's gift of help and assurance, incomplete in respect to the world. World and sacrament are meant to be one, for *world is ritual*—our world is a doing. A religion that enables man fully to relate himself to God must be a ritualistic one, for ritual and the world have the fullness of man's activity in common. Man knows his world through his body and he must express his religion through his body, too. In fact, that is what enables the whole world to become sacramental. To reduce religion to the contemplation of abstract, ethical principles is an attempt either to deform man or to ignore him as he actually exists.

The Incarnation, taken seriously for what it is, is the answer to our needs and the goal of our lives. The Incarnation is God's meaning embodied in the world. If we are true followers of Christ, *incorporated* into him, the physical embodiment of our love of God will be seen to be the only means we have for spiritual fulfillment. Living in Christ for what *he* is, the antithesis between "inner-outer," "secular-religious," will be overcome. As created by God, we ourselves are the overcoming of this antithesis, for, as we have seen, our being as persons is being-in-the-world: the outward expression of ourselves in the world is the only means by which we can have an intimate, personal life with God. It is the only way we can have *any* kind of life with him. If we offer ourselves to the Father, telling him with our whole lives that we want to live in *his* world—that is, the world of Christ—we will in *that* action be creating our world the way he wants us to; no additional action or complicated intention on our part is necessary. Genuinely Christian lives are astoundingly simple. Christians always do something more merely by doing what they are doing: by doing *this* they are doing *that*, by living the sacraments they are creating the world, by creating the world they are loving God the way he wants them to. That is the fulfillment God makes available for us by putting us in the universe.

I am struck by the similarity of the conclusions we have drawn with certain conclusions found in the thought of Pierre Teilhard de Chardin. Both positions stress that Christianity is progressive, active, forward looking. Both stress the present incompleteness of the world and the world's need for man's creative action in it.

Father Teilhard's language is that of hopeful evolution; it locates our lives in terms of the total development of the universe and consequently gives cosmic significance to our most insignificant-appearing activities. It is the duty of a sick person, for example, to fight to regain his health with every means available to him, but if and when such struggle cannot achieve its purpose, the resignation which follows still plays a significant role in the cosmic transformation he helps to bring about. Because Teilhard expresses himself in vivid, material terms, the progress and hope he describes have immediate appeal for us. There has been material progress in the evolution of the universe, and to be able to locate oneself as an important agent in that continuing adventure is to have something solid upon which to base one's life. Teilhard himself said that his thought encouraged people because it supplied "a perspective where the past, the present, and the future meet in an atmosphere of material progress and progressing love."[3]

Father Teilhard is an attractive person; we feel we know him intimately through his theoretical works as well as through his letters and the reminiscences of his friends because he was genuinely himself in all that he did. His love as a boy for the *hardest* objects he could find, pieces of iron especially, offers us a significant insight into his nature. He loved tangible things and he learned to express himself in tangible terms; he saw spirit in matter and the mystical Christ throughout the universe. Everything in the universe is somehow one and is developing toward the One who is also its Source.

Father Teilhard's approach to man is based upon a special interpretation of the theory of evolution. His approach is theoretical although, as we have pointed out, it is often vivid because it

[3] Quoted in *Teilhard de Chardin: Pilgrim of the Future*, Neville Braybrooke, ed. (New York: Seabury Press, 1964), p. 48.

concerns the material world and is stated in compelling, material terms. In Teilhard's view consciousness is a universal property of matter, but one which is able specifically to reveal itself for what it is only where complexity is sufficiently developed: that is why man appeared so late in the evolutionary process. One of the weakest aspects of his system appears to be its questioned ability to recognize the force and reality of evil as Christianity has traditionally understood them.

The position I have taken does not depend in its origin upon the type of theoretical interpretations Teilhard makes, although there is nothing inherently hostile between my basic contentions and many of his views. The starting point of the position I have developed is our *most immediate experience of ourselves in our lived-world*. I have tried to suggest an analysis of ourselves as we empirically exist in the present—the starting point for all of our theories, even those of evolution—and from that analysis we have come to conclusions strikingly like Teilhard's. Examining our most immediate relation to reality, we have found that our being is itself the embodiment of time; the latter's dynamism is one with us. As we are most immediately related to the reality around us, which reality we know is not exhausted by the horizon of our already-known world, we see that our being is *task* and *project*. For somewhat different reasons, but with the force of our whole analysis behind it, we join with Teilhard in concluding that man must create. In our view, too, man must use the universe in order to be himself; in his use of it he is *spiritualizing* it, but the meaning we draw from that term does not depend upon some of the special claims Teilhard makes.

Both views agree that some kind of conscious personality is the beginning and end of all things. Both agree with the primacy of community and our mutual dependence upon each other. When his spiritual insights are separated from his more speculative opinions, Father Teilhard's words are some of the most incisive I can find to say what I am trying to say. Father Teilhard believes that "each one of our works . . . contributes to perfect Christ in His mystical totality . . . In fact, through the unceasing operation of the Incarnation, the divine so thoroughly permeates all our creaturely energies that, in order to encounter and embrace it, we could not find a more appropriate milieu than that of our action."[4]

Every moment of our lives will assume supreme importance for us if, with Teilhard, we realize that "the intimacy of our union with Him is in fact a function of the exact fulfilment of the least of our tasks. We ought to accustom ourselves to this basic truth till we are steeped in it, until it becomes as familiar to us as the perception of relief or the reading of words. God . . . is not withdrawn from us beyond the tangible sphere; He is waiting for us at every moment in our action, in our work of the moment."[5] We should see "with a wave of joy that *the divine omnipresence* translates itself within our universe by the network of the organising forces of the total Christ. God exerts pressure, in us and upon us . . . only in the act of forming and consummating Christ who saves and suranimates the world. And since, in the course of this operation, Christ Himself does not act as a dead or passive point of convergence, but as a centre of radiation for the energies which lead the universe back to God through His humanity, the layers of divine action finally come to us impregnated with His organic energies.

". . . As a consequence of the Incarnation, the divine immensity has transformed itself for us into *the omnipresence of christification*."[6] Wherever we are, to use Teilhard's terms, we are "christifying" the universe; that is the way, to put it in our terms, the universe becomes *God's world*. We can participate in such wonderful work because

in Christ our consolation overflows.

[4] Pierre Teilhard de Chardin, *The Divine Milieu: an Essay on the Interior Life* (New York: Harper & Row, 1960), p. 31.
[5] *Ibid.*, p. 33.
[6] *Ibid.*, p. 101.

Index